Basic Internet for Busy Librarians

A Quick Course for Catching Up

Laura K. Murray

American Library Association
Chicago and London   1998

While extensive effort has gone into ensuring the reliability of information appearing in this book, the publisher makes no warranty, express or implied, on the accuracy or reliability of the information, and does not assume and hereby disclaims any liability to any person for any loss or damage caused by errors or omissions in this publication.

Trademarked names appear in the text of this book. Rather than identify or insert a trademark symbol at the appearance of each name, the authors and the American Library Association state that the names are used for editorial purposes exclusively, to the ultimate benefit of the owners of the trademarks. There is absolutely no intention of infringement on the rights of the trademark owners.

Project editor: Joan A. Grygel

Text design by Clarinda Publication Services

Composition in Goudy, ITC Legacy Sans and Willow using QuarkXpress 3.32 by the dotted i

Printed on 50-pound Arbor, a pH-neutral stock, and bound in 10-point coated cover stock by Edwards Brothers

The paper used in this publication meets the minimum requirements of American National Standard for Information Sciences—Permanence of Paper for Printed Library Materials, ANSI Z39.48-1992.∞

Library of Congress Cataloging-in-Publication Data
Murray, Laura K.
   Basic Internet for busy librarians : a quick course for catching up / Laura K. Murray.
      p.   cm.
   ISBN 0-8389-0725-3
   1. Internet (Computer network)—United States.   2. Library information networks—United States.   I. Title.Z674.75.I58M87   1998
   004.67'8—dc21   98-14067

Printed in the United States of America.

02 01 00 99 98   5 4 3 2 1

To James, Jeannette, Liz, and Mark
for your unwavering support,
encouragement, and love

Contents

Acronyms

ASCII	American Standard Code for Information Interchange
CSMA/CD	Carrier Sense Multiple Action with Collision Detection
CSU/DSU	Channel Service Unit/Data Service Unit
DNS	domain name server
FAQ	frequently asked questions
FTP	File Transfer Protocol
.gif	Graphic Interchange Format
HTML	HyperText Markup Language
http	HyperText Transport Protocol
IDG	Internet discussion groups
IP	Internet Protocol
IRC	Internet Relay Chat
ISDN	Integrated Services Digital Network
ISP	Internet service provider
.jpg	Joint Photographic Experts Group
KB	kilobytes
Kbps	kilobits per second
LAN	local area network
Mpbs	megabits per second
PACS-L	Public Access Computer Systems Forum
POP	Post Office Protocol
PPP/SLIP	Point to Point Protocol/Serial Line Internet Protocol
rn	read news
SGML	Standardized General Markup Language
SMTP	Simple Mail Transfer Protocol
TCP/IP	Transmission Control Protocol/Internet Protocol
URL	Uniform Resource Locator
WAIS	Wide Area Information Server
WWW	World Wide Web
WYSIWYG	what you see is what you get

Preface

The Internet offers a new way of doing almost everything in libraries. In reference departments, it is used for accessing online databases and ready-reference information. Technical services imports and exports bibliographic records using Internet protocols and cabling. Online catalogs are made available via Internet hypertext interfaces or terminal emulation applications. Professional development and interlibrary communication is often e-mail based.

As a teacher of continuing education workshops and a three-credit graduate course about the Internet, I am in touch with the dire need of so many present and future librarians to understand and use the Internet. I worry about the people behind the names on the inevitable and long waiting lists for my classes. What are their alternatives? It is my goal that this book provides a good answer to that question.

Bookstores offer dozens of large books covering the Internet from soup to nuts. The books are hundreds of pages long and weigh enough to build biceps when carried around. I've read them and lugged them, and I know whereof I speak. So many working librarians and other information professionals have little or no time to wade through a comprehensive tome about the Internet. So much learning is piecemeal and OTJ (on the job).

Basic Internet for Busy Librarians is just that: basic. You get a conceptual, nontechie definition and explanation of each aspect of the Internet and some hands-on exercises to help solidify the concepts. The process is fast. You can get through quite a bit of a chapter during a lunch hour and probably can finish it up during the next. (Just be careful not to spill your lunch on the keyboard.) Learning about the Internet and using it effectively do not have to be stressful, time-consuming, or overwhelming endeavors.

The lingo of the Internet can be intimidating to newbies (a new Internet user). Each chapter defines the jargon within. A list of acronyms following the contents will help you get past the alphabet soup of Internet-related terms.

Exercise steps are numbered for your convenience in following the sequence. Keys to press, items to click on, and exact wording to type are **boldfaced** (or boldfaced and **underlined** in the case of links) to help you see at a glance what to do. The majority of the exercises are hands-on, as denoted by a symbol of two hands. The exercises that serve only as examples do not have the hands-on symbol. Boxed copy, often within an exercise, is optional information that may not apply to your particular software or hardware situation.

I created the hands-on exercises with the latest (as of this publication date) versions of Windows 95, Netscape 4, and Internet Explorer. Because there are so many versions of Windows, Netscape, Internet Explorer, and other Internet software currently in use, it is improbable that you will be able to exactly reproduce the exercises offered in this book. When you find discrepancies, just look at the next step in the exercise, and you will be able to continue. Variety and variability are the nature of the Internet, and adjusting to that reality is part of the learning process.

Once you've completed this quick-start guide, you may wish to turn to one of those biceps-building Internet books as a reference source. I hope this book will take its place next to it on your shelf—but only after its pages are well-thumbed and dog-eared.

Finally, I give my sincere thanks to my editor, Patrick Hogan, for his inspiration, and to Meredith Case, for finding all the bugs in the exercises.

Making an
Exercises Directory

MAKING A FOLDER ON YOUR C: DRIVE

For Windows 95 or NT Users

To follow the exercises in this book without confusion, you should create a folder on your [C:] drive named *busy* in which to store your exercises.

1. start Windows Explorer
2. click on the **C:** drive in the left window
3. make sure the title of the right window is **Contents of '[C:]'**

> **HINT** *If the title of the right window is* not: **Contents of '[C:]'**, *click on the* **C:** *drive icon again.*

4. click on **File** in the menu bar
5. click on **New**

6. click on **Folder**

7. name the new folder **busy**

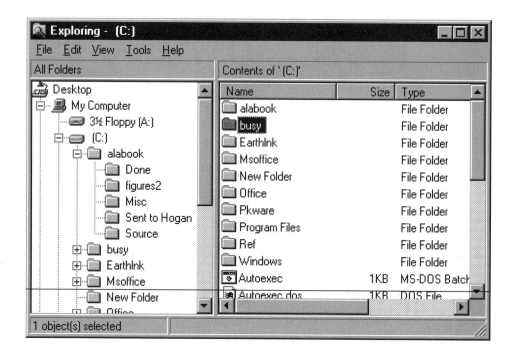

For Windows 3.1 Users

To follow the exercises in this book without confusion, you should create a folder on your C: drive named *busy* in which to store your exercises.

EXERCISE

1. double-click on your **Main** or **Accessories** group icon in your **Program Manager** window

2. double-click on the **File Manager** icon to start File Manager

3. locate the **C:** drive and directory (folder) in the left window

4. double-click on it to open **C:** (the root directory)

File Manager - [C:*.*]		

File   **Disk**   **Tree**   **View**   **Options**   **Send**   **Window**   **Help**

a   c   f   g   h   i   l   m   o   p   q

u   v   w   x   y   z   C: [MS-DOS_6]

c:\

acroread	monop	sierra
aldo	mouse	spirs
atmapps	msoffice	sr2
back	nancy	temp
boot-cfg	nancy1	tmp
colorman	net	trivia
cow	netback	utils
dev	netscap2	wilsonp
disclit	netscape	winapp
dlink	nwclient	winbacl
dos	oclc	window

5. look at the right window, make sure the title bar says **Contents of C:**

6. click on **File** in the menu bar

7. click on **Create Directory**

8. in the dialog box provided, type the directory name **busy**

Create Directory	

Current Directory: C:\

Name: busy

OK

Cancel

Help

9. click **OK**

10. click on **File** in the menu bar again

11. click on **Exit**

An Overview
at Top Speed

JUST WHAT IS THE INTERNET?

If you watch the evening news, the Internet is a chat room where evil preys upon innocents. If you watch commercial films, the Internet is a method of stealing classified government information or transferring millions of dollars into Swiss bank accounts from unlikely settings such as the beach or a high-speed commuter train. If you work in a library, the Internet is where your users will turn for fast, full-text information, many believing that cyberspace is the best source for *all* research. The truth is that the Internet can be used for all of the above. The reality is that the Internet is fairly simple to define. It is the *use* of the Internet that can get complicated.

SOME QUICK DEFINITIONS

Internet The Internet is millions of different computers communicating over copper and fiberoptic telecommunications cables that encircle the earth. They communicate using the same protocol, or language, called TCP/IP. Information is entered through a computer keyboard into a computer running TCP/IP software and is sent out through a modem or a network cable to a destination across the street, state, country, or continent. That's it. The challenge is to understand the myriad ways this global network can be used to deliver, receive, retrieve, and organize information.

Cybrarians

Cyber-librarians, or cybrarians, are the new breed of information specialists who are savvy about the Internet and online information and the hardware and software that make it tick. The reality is that every kind of information specialist, from interlibrary loan assistants to library directors, needs to understand the Internet. Why? It is the method of choice for information management, distribution, and communication. Today's cybrarians caught the Internet wave as the tide was coming in. Tomorrow's cybrarians must simply learn how to swim and, perhaps, take some surfing lessons in preparation for the next wave of innovation.

The most challenging part of learning about the Internet is understanding the alphabet soup of acronyms that create the unique lexicon needed to travel in cyberspace. Let's jump right in, eyes wide open, and see if we can swim.

TCP/IP   This is where it all begins. *TCP/IP* stands for Transmission Control Protocol/Internet Protocol. This is the software that allows a computer to communicate with other computers on the Internet regardless of differences between hardware and software. TCP/IP software *must* be installed on any computer if you wish to achieve full access to the Internet or offer (serve) information on the Internet. (You can, however, access the Internet in a text-only mode without TCP/IP by using the Internet connection of a mainframe computer. See Shell Accounts in chapter 2.) TCP/IP is actually a suite of applications and protocols. (A *protocol* is a program that establishes a consistent standard of communication between computers running it.)

FTP   FTP, or File Transfer Protocol, is part of the TCP/IP suite. FTP allows a computer with an Internet connection to connect to other computers and download (retrieve) and upload (send) their files from remote locations anywhere in the world. (It's easier than mailing a floppy disk or CD-ROM.) See chapter 7 for the detailed scoop on FTP.

Telnet   Telnet is an application that allows those with an Internet connection to connect to and use programs on another computer connected to the Internet. Many online library catalogs are available via Telnet. Telnet allows anyone in the world with an Internet connection to access and search the Library of Congress online catalog (and Harvard, and Yale, and so on). See chapter 6 for the entire Telnet story.

Web Browsers

Beyond the core of TCP/IP, FTP, and Telnet, there are important applications that access information on the Internet in a variety of ways.

The most diverse and popular access method is via a World Wide Web browser. The most popular WWW browsers are Netscape Communication's Netscape and Microsoft's Internet Explorer. A Web browser allows you to access information on the Internet in a variety of formats: text, graphics, sound, and motion picture files are all potentially viewable and retrievable through a Web browser. You can also Telnet and FTP through a browser; see chapter 3 for an in-depth explanation.

E-mail and Chatting

E-mail (or electronic mail) programs allow you to send messages to anyone with an Internet e-mail account. Commonly used e-mail programs are Netscape Mail and Microsoft Office mail. You may also participate in ongoing discussion lists devoted to a particular topic. Discussion lists exist for every kind of information professional and specialty: reference specialists, archivists, catalogers, support staff, medical librarians, and business librarians; the list is delightfully extensive.

Gopher and Friends

Some once-popular, but now fading, Internet stars are Gopher and its relatives: Veronica and Jughead. Gopher is a menu interface to Internet resources. Veronica and Jughead are tools for searching Gopher menus and resources. Chapter 9 talks a bit more about these obsolete cyber-rodents.

HOW IT IS ALL CONNECTED

There are "backbones" of high-speed telecommunications cables all over the globe. Tapping into these backbones are the Internet service providers. The end user then gains access to the Internet through the service provider.

Addresses: Numbers and Names

Everyone connecting directly to the Internet (see chapter 2 for details on connectivity) must be assigned a unique IP (Internet Protocol) address. These addresses are four sets of numbers separated by periods, for example: 141.254.10.9.

Because names are easier to remember than numbers, these addresses are assigned domain names that are registered in a domain-name server (DNS). When someone tries to access your IP address using its domain name, the DNS translates the name back into its unique IP address to make the connection. For example, the IP address 141.254.10.9 could be assigned the domain-name address: mycomputer.library.mycollege.edu.

CATCHING YOUR BREATH

You have just cruised through an overview of the Internet at the speed of a Porsche on a Montana highway. Let's pull over to the side of the road and take stock:

TCP/IP (Transmission Control Protocol/Internet Protocol) is the software suite that allows computers to connect to the Internet. It is the heart of the Internet.

FTP (File Transfer Protocol) is the protocol that allows files of any type to be sent or received over the Internet.

Telnet is the application that allows a computer to act like a terminal and connect to remote computers and use their programs, such as online library catalogs or games.

Web browsers are programs that allow access to interactive documents and multimedia information (the World Wide Web) and can also serve as all-purpose interfaces to the entire Internet.

Other topics covered in coming chapters are the creation of World Wide Web documents and searching the Internet.

Congratulations! You've just taken the first step toward becoming a cybrarian.

Plugging into
the Internet

TCP/IP (Transmission Control Protocol/Internet Protocol) is the software heart and soul of the Internet. When it runs under Microsoft
Windows, TCP/IP is described as a "stack" because, as with all other communications protocols, it is arranged in layers. There is a TCP layer that
handles delivering data correctly and without errors. Then the IP layer
is responsible for moving packets of data from one point to another.
Each packet is identified with a numeric IP address to get it to its destination. A sockets layer contains program subroutines that permit access
to TCP/IP.

TCP/IP comes as a suite that includes Telnet (a remote-access
application) and FTP (File Transfer Protocol for downloading and up-
loading files between computers on the Internet).

Just as paper tissues for blowing your nose may be called by the
brand name Kleenex, TCP/IP suites are labeled with a variety of brand
names. Microsoft Windows users can obtain it as Trumpet Winsock.
The Trumpet home page is located on the World Wide Web at http://
www.trumpet.com/dtwsk.htm. The file containing the TCP/IP stack is
called winsock.dll. It is often found in the c:\ windows directory. If
you have a Novell LAN, your TCP/IP suite may be disguised under the
name LAN Workplace.

Microsoft Windows 95 users get Microsoft's TCP/IP stack included
as a standard feature along with Telnet and FTP and the Windows
Explorer Web browser (see http://www.aa.net/~pcd/slp95faq.html for
Windows 95 TCP/IP setup instructions). Ditto for IBM's OS/2 Warp
operating system.

GETTING THE SOFTWARE

If you are not ready or able to upgrade to the latest version of your favorite operating system, you can easily acquire all the software you need in one bundle. Software bundles are an accessible and affordable way to get started connecting to the Internet. They usually include a Web browser (such as Netscape, which includes an e-mail application) and utilities for dialing your modem (if you are using one), in addition to TCP/IP, FTP, and Telnet. Your Internet service provider (ISP) should provide you with the Internet software you need or with an easy method of obtaining it. Commercial online services such as CompuServe, Prodigy, America Online, and Microsoft Network include most of the Internet software you need or make it available for free downloading.

CHOOSING AN INTERNET SERVICE PROVIDER

You purchase Internet connections and the necessary software and hardware from an Internet service provider (ISP). If you or someone you know has Internet access, you can get The List, a national list of Internet providers, from http://thelist.iworld.com. The List allows you to identify both large national ISPs and small local ISPs such as AlbanyNet for the Capital District of New York State. Following is the entry in The List for AlbanyNet.

AlbanyNet, Inc.

Area/Country Codes:	518
Automated email:	info@albany.net
Human email:	sales@albany.net
Phone:	(+1) (518) 462-6262 (9am–9pm M–F)
Fax:	(+1) (518) 463-0014
URL:	http://www.albany.net/
Services:	SLIP, PPP, ISDN 56K through T3 dedicated, corporate bandwidth mgmt.

Fees:	Dialup: Personal:
	    $13.89/mo for 15 hrs, then $0.91
	    $24.95/mo for unlimited usage +tx.
	Visit www.albany.net/Info for full pricing or contact sales@albany.net for a quote.

Added:	

Updated: 96.10.01

Notes:

Modem: Albany: +1 (518) 242-1111
                  Amsterdam: +1 (518) 246-1111
                  Saratoga/Glens Falls: +1 (518) 245-1111

Following are some suggested points to discuss with an Internet provider. First, tell the provider your needs.

Who will be using the Internet?

How many?

What tasks do you need to perform?

Next, tell the provider your current hardware configuration: Are you on a LAN (local area network), or are the PCs stand-alone?

How much does it cost for monthly, hourly, surcharges, storage, discounts, and toll-free access?

What type of direct connectivity is available, and how much is it?

What modem speeds are supported?

Does it cost more for high-speed modem use?

Is the dial-up number local or long distance?

Is connection through a packet carrier such as SprintNet?

If so, is there an additional charge for this carrier?

What are peak usage hours?

How long does it take to connect during peak hours? (Less than five minutes is good.)

Ask the provider for the capacity of its outgoing connection to the Internet. T1 is acceptable for a local system; T3 is appropriate for regional and national providers. Anything less than T1 should be avoided for an institutional account, but a provider with less than a T1 connection of its own could service a small number of customers and could work for a personal account. (You'll find out about T1 and T3 later in this chapter.)

Get a clear overview of the provider's various account packages and their costs. Match these to your list of needs. For example, the cheapest account may just offer e-mail, but for slightly more money you may be able to get an account that allows full graphical access and a choice of Internet access tools.

National Internet Providers

The heavy hitters in the provision of Internet services can be identified at Jay Barker's Online Connection, http://www.barkers.org/online/

index.html. This site presents well-organized information for major Internet service providers who, at the time of this writing, are AT&T WorldNet, Netcom, Prodigy Internet, SpryNet, America Online, CompuServe, Concentric, EarthLink, IBM Internet, MCI Internet, MindSpring, Microsoft Network, and Sprint Internet.

SERVICE	COST PER MONTH	HOURS INCLUDED	ADDITIONAL HOURS
AT&T WorldNet	$ 4.95	3	$2.50
	$19.95	Unlimited	N/A
Concentric	$ 7.95	5	$1.95
	$19.95	Unlimited	N/A
EarthLink	$19.95	Unlimited	N/A
IBM Internet	$ 4.95	3	$1.95
	$19.95	100*	$1.95*

*Effective April 1, 1998. Unlimited plan available until that time.

TYPES OF CONNECTIONS

There are two basic methods of connecting to the Internet:

directly, using Ethernet protocol

dial-up, using a modem and standard phone lines, or an ISDN (Integrated Services Digital Network) telecommunication line

ETHERNET DEFINED

Ethernet is the current standard in local area network technology. Data is transmitted in packets of bytes in a CSMA/CD (Carrier Sense Multiple Action with Collision Detection) arrangement. All the devices attached to a LAN "listen" for packet transmissions before attempting to transmit. If two do start to transmit simultaneously, one stops transmission and waits for the other.

Direct Connections: Fast and Efficient

There are backbones of high-speed network telecommunication cables covering the earth. These network cables branch, meet, and end at network access points. ISPs are the companies that sell access to the Internet. The ISPs tie into the high-speed Internet backbones at network access points using slower but more-numerous cables. Individuals and institutions purchase access to the Internet from Internet service providers. When purchasing a direct connection to the Internet (rather than a dial-up), you have a variety of options: 56 Kbps, frame relay, T1, and T3.

56 Kbps

The simplest type of direct connection is the 56 Kbps (kilobits per second) line. In essence, it is a phone line that directly connects to the ISP and is dedicated to the purpose of carrying your Internet transmissions. The speed at which a leased line conducts data is 56 Kbps.

You'll need some hardware in addition to the TCP/IP software suite to connect your computer to the leased line. Your Internet service provider can sell you the hardware you need as part of the installation cost. You'll need an Ethernet adaptor to make your computer send and receive data in the appropriate protocol. Minimally, beyond the adaptor, you'll need a router and a CSU/DSU (Channel Service Unit/Data Service Unit). A router routes the incoming data from the single leased line to a file server or multiple computers and makes sure the data packets get to where they need to go. A CSU/DSU manages all the nuances of the data traveling on the leased line such as signal frequency, speed, and density.

The cost of a leased line is calculated based on its location, the phone company, and the length of the actual phone line. Costs may vary widely depending on the telephone company, connection, and ISP. If frame relay (see below) is not available, this is the most reasonable type of direct connection.

Frame Relay

Another way to get a 56 Kbps connection is via frame relay. Essentially, each individual institution sends its data over a standard leased line to the phone company into a "frame cloud." These individual frame transmissions are then channeled into one high-speed line, such as a T1, to the Internet service provider. Therefore, frame relay is a cheaper direct connection because the ISP has to manage only one connection for many customers! Where frame relay is available, you have the option of leasing a 56 Kbps.

T1 Connections

A T1 line transmits data at 1.5 Mbps (megabits per second). These lines are fast and can handle a heavy data load. Often, this is the type of line an ISP uses to connect to the Internet; your ISP may be able to provide you with one as well. While the installation fee is comparable to that of a 56 Kbps leased line, the CSU/DSU costs significantly more due to the additional complexity of the T1 transmission; the monthly charges can be more than $600 per month. The cost is justified if your data transmission needs are heavy.

T3 Connections

A T3 connection carries roughly 45 Mbps, which is the equivalent of twenty-eight T1 lines. The Internet backbone is made up of this type of heavy-duty line. A large, sophisticated Internet service provider might use a T3 connection, or a very large institution with a heavy and frequent data load might use it.

Dial-Up Connections

Connecting directly to the Internet can cost too much for individuals or libraries with a small budget. Now that speedy modems cost less than $100, and unlimited connection time to Internet service providers is about $20 per month, a dial-up connection is an affordable and increasingly feasible option for any Internet user.

Modems

If you don't already have a modem, buy the highest speed modem you can afford. A modem that functions at 28.8 Kbps is the minimum speed recommended for Internet access. You need a special ISDN modem if you choose an ISDN line.

ISDN

ISDN (integrated services digital network) dial-up connections use standard phone lines. You get an ISDN connection from your local phone company. It allows you from 2 to 24 telecommunications channels on a single line, and the speed can be 64 to 128 Kbps. A basic service of two channels allows you to connect a special ISDN phone and your computer to the same line and run them simultaneously.

If your phone company offers ISDN service, the cost starts at around $30 per month. The biggest expense is the ISDN software needed to connect your computer to the ISDN line, minimally about $2,000. As more phone companies offer ISDN and connection and hardware costs decrease, it *may* become the connection method of choice for home and small business users.

Shell Accounts

If you as an individual or your institution wants a readily accessible and inexpensive connection to the Internet, you have two basic choices: a shell account or a PPP/SLIP (Point to Point Protocol/Serial Line Internet Protocol) account. These types of accounts usually range in price from $10 to $20 per month, and all you need is a modem to take advantage of them.

A shell account is the cheapest and most bare-bones way to get connected. You are given a phone number to dial into your Internet provider's computer. You need telecommunications software (such as ProComm, Crosstalk, or Telix) to make the connection. Sometimes your Internet provider offers the telecommunications software as part of your account package. Once you dial your assigned number, you log onto a host computer and use its connection to "get" to the Internet. Your computer acts as a dumb terminal and lets the host computer do its "thinking" for it. Unless your Internet provider offers utilities such as SlipKnot and The Internet Adaptor on its shell account computer server that you dial into, you are limited to only text information on the Internet and cannot take advantage of the graphical wonders of the World Wide Web.

Free-nets

Many public Free-nets offer Internet access and e-mail via shell accounts. This may be the simplest and cheapest way to get started. You can find a comprehensive list of Free-nets at http://www.commerce.com/net2/internet/bbs/freebbs_top.html.

SLIP and PPP

Point to Point Protocol was developed after SLIP. These are communications protocols that allow a computer to directly access the Internet using a high-speed modem that is connected to a SLIP or PPP server. These protocols work with TCP/IP software installed on your computer. The connection is made over telephone lines. Your ISP should offer you a local number to dial and rates that match your budget. To make these types of connections you need a computer, a modem of 28.8 Kbps or higher, SLIP and TCP/IP software, and an account on a SLIP server.

The benefit of SLIP/PPP connectivity is that you can choose which Internet tools and utilities you wish to install and run on your local computer. You can install your choice of e-mail programs, WWW clients, and Telnet and FTP protocols. You are in charge of how you search the Internet.

GETTING AN INTERNET SERVICE PROVIDER

EXERCISE

HINT	*You'll need to borrow someone else's Internet connection and browser to visit The List of Internet service providers and select one for your own account.*

1. create a formatted floppy disk to receive the ISP software you'll be downloading

2. pop that formatted disk in the floppy drive now

3. when through with the exercise, take the ISP software saved on the disk back to your own computer for installation

Using The List to Establish an Account with EarthLink

In the following exercise, you obtain a PPP account through EarthLink. The exercise uses EarthLink as its ISP of choice. EarthLink covers a very broad territory and may be a feasible first choice for you as well.

EXERCISE

Note: These steps work with either Netscape or Internet Explorer

1. start your browser

2. in *Netscape,* click in the **Net Site:** or **Location:** box under the toolbar

   OR

   in *Internet Explorer,* click in the **Address** box

3. type **http://thelist.internet.com**

4. press the **ENTER** key to open the connection

5. click on **locate an ISP by area code**

HINT	*You can locate an ISP by other characteristics such as country code.*

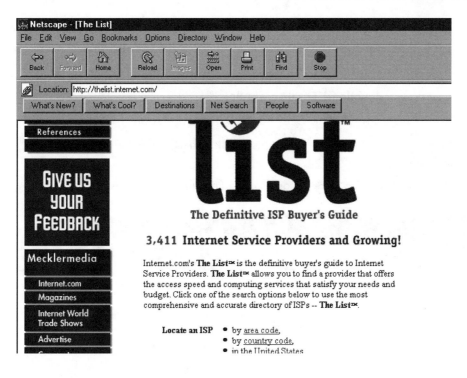

6. scroll down in the table provided

7. locate your state name

8. click on your area code in your state

9. click on the link **EarthLink Network**

10. click on the **Web Site** URL link

11. once you connect to their home page, click on the **Join EarthLink** graphic

12. click on the **TotalAccess** link (it may be far down the page)

13. click on the **download TotalAccess** link

    Note: This is an FTP site. See chapter 7 for more about FTP.

14. click on the appropriate TotalAccess link, whether it is Windows 3.1, 95, or Macintosh

15. you should see the **Save As** dialog box (note the file name)

Save As...	? ×

Save in: 📁 busy

File name: ta95v142   Save

Save as type: All Files (*.*)   Cancel

16. switch to the **3½ Floppy** icon folder

17. click on the **Save** button to activate the download

> **HINT** *Your download of the TotalAccess software could take a while, so you may want to get away from your computer for a break!*

 EXERCISE

When the download is done, continue with the following steps at your own computer.

1. go to your own computer and turn it on

2. open Windows Explorer

3. click on the **C:** drive in the left window

4. double-click on the **busy** folder to open it

5. click on **File** in the menu bar

6. click on **New**

7. click on **Folder**

8. name the new folder **ISP**

9. locate the **3½ Floppy** icon in the left window and click on it once

10. in the right window, you should see the name of the file you downloaded

11. in the left window, locate your **ISP** folder under your **busy** folder

12. click on the downloaded file in the right window and drag it to the **ISP** folder in the left window to copy it from the floppy to the hard drive

13. double-click on the **ISP** folder in the left window, note the file you just copied to it

14. double-click on the file you just copied to ISP, for example: **tav142**

15. the files extract themselves

16. in the left window, locate the **Setup** application icon and double-click on it

You can call EarthLink toll-free and receive your account name and password immediately as long as you have your credit card handy. Its number is (800) 395-8425.

17. click on **Yes** if you wish to set up an account online, rather than by phone (if you don't wish to establish an EarthLink account by phone, click on **No** [you don't wish to set up an account online], then the **Next** button)

18. enter the information EarthLink requires to establish an account

19. read the **Enduser/Subscriber** agreement and click on the **I Agree** button

The TotalAccess software should automatically recognize your modem type and put in the proper settings that were established when you set up your account. You click on the Modem Settings button to familiarize yourself with the settings.

20. click on **Next** and the software dials an 800 number to retrieve your EarthLink account information

21. scroll through the list of dial-up numbers to find the one that is local to you

22. once you click on your local number, you should get a **Registration Is Complete** dialog box

23. click on **Next**

24. if you are prompted to install Netscape (and you don't have it already) click on **Yes** and you are walked through the Netscape installation

25. when asked to configure "automatic dialing and hangup" click on **Yes**

    You may receive an instruction dial box like this:

You may then receive instructions for starting Netscape:

> ## Instructions
>
> > Start Netscape.
>
> 1. Click the Start item on the Windows 95 toolbar.
>
> 2. Highlight the Programs item.
>
> 3. Highlight the TotalAccess
>
> 4. Click the Netscape icon.
>
> [Next >]   [Ignore]

26. click on **Next**

    You may receive a dialog box like this:

> ## Instructions
>
> > Congratulations!
>
> You are now on the Internet using TotalAccess!
>
> 1. Don't forget to disconnect from EarthLink Network when you're done.
>
> [OK]

27. minimize or exit your open windows until you see your desktop

28. double-click on the **Shortcut to EarthLink** (it was automatically created)

29. enter your password and click on the **Save Password** check box

30. click on **Connect**

    You should get a confirmation that you are connected. If you did not install Netscape from the TotalAccess setup, you can start it as you always have. If you did install Netscape from the TotalAccess setup, the steps are:

    a. click on the **Start** button

    b. click on the **TotalAccess** folder

    c. click on **Netscape**

Addresses for Commercial Online Services

America Online, CompuServe, Microsoft Network, and Prodigy are commonly used online service providers that offer gateways to the Internet. You can visit their sites for an overview of services at the following addresses.

America Online
http://www.aol.com/

CompuServe
http://world.compuserve.com/

Microsoft Network
http://www.msn.com/default.asp

Prodigy
http://www.prodigy.com/

The advantages of using an online service for Internet access are that it is quick and easy to set up an account, the interfaces are usually very user friendly, and you can access non-Internet online products offered by the service. The disadvantages include heavy traffic and sometimes unreliable connections to the Internet.

PARING DOWN AND PLUGGING IN

An Internet service provider, or ISP, provides you with your connection to the Internet and (usually) the software you may need to create and use this connection. You can find a list of ISPs at The List Web site (http://thelist.internet.com). There are direct connections that are appropriate for institutional use: 56 Kbps, frame relay, T1, and T3 are common choices. Connection is also possible through a modem, and you have the choice of a very fast ISDN modem line or dialing your modem into a SLIP or PPP server controlled by your ISP.

SLIP and PPP connections are the affordable way to get flexible and sophisticated Internet access at a low cost and are an excellent choice for an individual. When selecting an ISP and choosing a type of connection, don't be afraid to ask lots of questions: That's the best way to understand your options and match your needs to the available services.

The easiest way to get connected is through a commercial online service such as America Online, Prodigy, CompuServe, or Microsoft Network. If you have a modem, all you need to do is slip the free disk they all provide (floppy or CD-ROM) in your computer and click on the designated installation file. You are then gently walked through all the necessary steps to getting plugged into the Internet.

Browsing, Bookmarking, and Surfing the World Wide Web

3

THE WORLD WIDE WEB DEFINED

Every day, newcomers to the Internet enter libraries seeking a chance to plug into cyberspace. Neophytes are sometimes puzzled by the differentiation made between the World Wide Web (WWW) and the "rest of the Internet." This explanation can perhaps smooth the brows of those eager to put it all in place.

Web documents are formatted in a standard call HyperText Markup Language, or HTML. Hypertext contains links to other documents and information in a variety of formats including multimedia types such as graphics, motion picture, and sound files.

Two software tools make connection to the Web possible: the servers and the browsers. A WWW server runs special WWW server software. This software allows information to be presented in a hypertext format; therefore, it is called HyperText Transport Protocol or http. It also allows other computers on the Internet to connect to the server and access the hypertext information.

Computers running WWW server software and the hypertext documents they contain compose the World Wide Web.

The second part to this picture is the WWW browsers (for example, Netscape, Internet Explorer, or Lynx). Browsers are designed specifically to connect to WWW servers and display hypertext information and their associated links and multimedia file formats.

WWW browsers can also connect to Gopher, FTP, and Telnet sites. Such sites are *not* the World Wide Web. That's why it gets confusing. You can use your Web browser to connect to World Wide Web servers *and* the rest of the Internet. How do you know when you are *not* connecting your WWW browser to the WWW? The answer is: check your URL.

ANATOMY OF A URL

The addresses you use to connect to Internet sites through your browser are called Uniform Resource Locators or URLs. The components of a URL are

scheme://host.domain/path/filename

The URL *scheme* is your clue to what type of information you will find at an address. If the scheme is http, you are connecting to the World Wide Web server. If it is anything else, you are connecting to the rest of the Internet. For example:

http://lcweb.loc.gov:80 (Library of Congress WWW home page)

gopher://marvel.loc.gov:90 (the Library of Congress Gopher menu)

ftp://ftp.netscape.com (the Netscape FTP site)

A single computer can run WWW server software as well as software for other information accessed via Telnet, FTP, and Gopher. Hence, a single computer can be part of the World Wide Web and part of the rest of the Internet.

Beyond Schemes

You know what a scheme is, now let's address the other components using this sample URL for the site Libweb—Libraries on the Web: USA—Academic. Its URL is

http://sunsite.berkeley.edu/Libweb/usa-acad.html

The Host position on the URL tells you the name of the computer on which the file is located. The host computer in this example is sunsite.

After the host name comes the domain name(s) (see chapter 1) for the institution or company (and sometimes a department within the institution). In this example *berkeley* indicates that the institution is Berkeley. The domain is .edu for education. Other domain names used on the Internet are

mil   military sites

gov   nonmilitary government sites

org   organizations (usually nonprofit)

com   commercial organizations

net   networks

edu   educational

After the domain comes the path, which is the directory(ies) in which the file is located. The directory in this example is libweb.

The File position in the URL is the file name itself. The file name in the example is usa-acad.html. The extension of .html or .htm tells us its format is HyperText Markup Language.

HINT   *URLs can be case sensitive. If you see a URL that uses capital letters, don't ignore them.*

BROWSERS

The most popular browsers, Netscape and Internet Explorer, are graphical browsers that allow you to see pictures and other graphical enhancements to a hypertext file. When configured appropriately, Netscape also allows you to see motion picture and hear audio files. Internet Explorer needs no additional configuration to support these file types.

Lynx, another browser, is text-only and is still found mainly in academic mainframe environments. The limitation of Lynx is that users cannot view pictures or hear sound. Some libraries still choose Lynx over graphical browsers because text loads more quickly than visual or sound files and because library users cannot locate or download illegal visual materials and are less likely to tie up Internet workstations with recreational activities.

Home Pages

Every browser has a designated default home page. A home page is a hypertext document that is an introduction to other hypertext resources. Hypertext documents are called pages, even if they are very long. There are no actual page breaks in hypertext documents, which makes each individual document one page, no matter how lengthy it is.

Every browser comes with a default setting that points to the home page for its publisher. You can easily change your default home page to connect to any Web server you wish.

More about HyperText Markup Language

As stated previously, Web pages are formatted using HyperText Markup Language, or HTML. Hypertext documents therefore have a file extension of .html or .htm. HTML documents are plain ASCII (American Standard Code for Information Interchange) text, meaning that any word processing software or any text editor can understand them. HTML works by placing tags in the document that let the browser know how to display the text or connect to another Web or Internet resource. Tags are placed in angle brackets to differentiate them from plain-text characters. For example:

<b>This text will be bolded.</b>

The <b> and </b> are HTML tags that instruct the browser to make the text **boldfaced** in between the two tags. Another example is

<i> This text will be italicized. </i>

All the readers of the document containing these tags see is: **This text will be bolded.** *This text will be italicized.*

For more details on HTML and its tags, see chapter 4.

Sampling Browsers

There are a variety of ways you can sample graphical browsers, if you are in the position of having to make a choice. (On the other hand, you may simply be given one where you work or as part of your home Internet access.) You can download browsers directly from their developers' home pages or from a variety of sites. Following is a quick tour of Netscape and Internet Explorer.

Netscape and Internet Explorer

Your first task is to get to know the basic elements of the Netscape menu and toolbars. Let's look at them in the order you need to know them using the following sample exercise. Surfing the World Wide Web refers to the action of starting at a known site, then following the links leading from that site wherever they may take you. Following is an exercise in controlled surfing, sort of a boogie-board approach for the beginner.

 EXERCISE

This exercise works with both Netscape and Internet Explorer. You will visit the American Library Association home page.

1. start your browser

HINT   *You are at the default home page for the browser you selected. This page varies, but if Netscape was installed without any modifications, it will be the Netscape Communications Corporation's home page (http:// home.netscape.com). If Internet Explorer is not modified, you see its home page (http://home.microsoft.com).*

HINT

To leave the home page, you can follow links that are part of that page, or you can tell your browser another URL to which you want to connect.

2. in *Netscape,* click in the **Location:** box under the toolbar

OR

in *Internet Explorer,* click in the **Address** box

3. type the URL: **http://www.ala.org**

  If the scheme is http:, you do not have to type it in because Netscape and Internet Explorer will assume you want to connect to an http server.

4. press the **ENTER** key to open the connection

HINT *When the Netscape browser is in the process of connecting to a site or loading a document, stars (or meteors or whatever) shoot in the N icon in the upper right corner of the window. When Internet Explorer is in the process of connecting, the E/world icon in the upper right corner of its window revolves. Both browsers show the progress of the connection in the bottom bar of the window as well.*

The ALA home page may look like this:

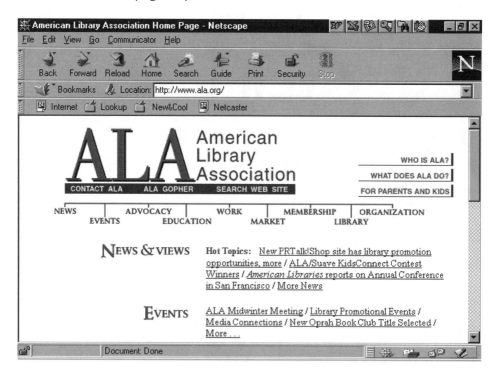

5. click on the link **Who is ALA?** (or a similar link)

HINT	*When you place your mouse point on an active link in an HTML document, it turns into a hand. If you place your pointer on something that appears to be a link and the hand does not appear, it's not a link. Links used in exercises appear **boldfaced** and <u>underlined</u>.*

You now see a second page. You are no longer viewing the ALA home page.

6. scroll down the page

7. click on **What does ALA do?** (or a similar link)

8. click on the **Advocating** link (or a similar link)

    Imagine you wish to take another quick look at the previous page.

9. click on the **Back** button to move to the previous screen

10. click on the **Forward** button to return to the page where you were

    Imagine you want to return to this page again and again.

11. in *Netscape,* click on the **Bookmark** menu heading

    click **Add Bookmark**

    click on the **Bookmark** menu heading again

    You should see the link you added appear in the Bookmarks list.

OR

in *Internet Explorer,* click on the **Favorites** button

click on **Add to Favorites**

click the **OK** button in the confirmation dialog box

click on the **Favorites** button again to the link added to the list

You should see the link you added appear in the **Favorites** list.

BOOKMARKS AND FAVORITES

In Netscape, you can create a bookmark for any site on the Web that you want to visit again. When you choose Add Bookmark from the Bookmark menu, the URL for the site you are viewing is added to a list of bookmarks that is stored in a file on your hard drive called bookmark.htm. You can view your bookmarks at any time by pulling down the Bookmark menu.

Internet Explorer allows you to save URLs to a Favorites menu. The URLs are actually stored as shortcuts in a folder called Favorites when you choose Add to Favorites from the menu. You can see your favorites in a list when you pull down the Favorites menu.

Bookmarks and Favorites are great tools for reference librarians. When a site is located once to answer a library user's question, you can bookmark or save it as a favorite. The next time the question is asked, you can find the answer with just a few mouse clicks on the Bookmark or Favorites list.

---

12. scroll down to the **National Library Week** link (or a similar link)

13. click on the link once

HINT   *Imagine that you want to save a document to your local disk so you can open it in a word processor and copy and paste direct quotes from it. The next part of this exercise instructs you to save your files to the busy folder on your C: drive. If you did not yet create the busy folder, turn to Making an Exercise Folder for instructions.*

14. click on **File** in the menu bar

15. in *Netscape,* click on **Save As**; a Save As dialog box should appear

    OR

    in *Internet Explorer,* click on **Save As File**; a Save As dialog box should appear

HINT	*Notice the file name. You can rename a file to any name you wish.*

16. click on the **File name text box**

17. replace the old name with a new one: **alainfo**

18. click on the **Save as type** list box

    Your choices for saving an HTML file with HTML tags are Source or HTML in Netscape or HTML in Internet Explorer. To save it as a generic ASCII text file without the HTML tags, your choices are Text in Netscape or Plain Text in Internet Explorer.

19. click on the **Text File** (or **Plain Text**) choice

    Notice the default drive and directory where the file will be saved. It can be C:\netscape. for *Netscape,* or C:\windows for *Internet Explorer.*

20. change the **Save in** location to the C: drive (to take you to the root directory of C:)

21. locate and double-click on the **busy** folder to open it

22. click **OK**

    Bravo! You have just completed a visit to the ALA Web site and have downloaded an HTML file to your C: drive as text. You can open the text file you just downloaded with your favorite word processor or Windows notepad, then edit and print it.

SAVING PICTURE (GRAPHIC) FILES

Netscape and Internet Explorer automatically display picture files that have a .gif (Graphic Interchange Format) extension at the end of their file names (for example: dog.gif could be a picture of a dog). Another file type these browsers automatically recognize is .jpg (Jpeg), which is a modified .gif file.

In both Netscape and Internet Explorer you can save (download) a picture file by pointing to the image as you see it on the screen and clicking on the right mouse button. When you do this, you see a menu with the choice Save Image As in Netscape or Save Picture As in Explorer.

When you click on Save Image As or Save Picture As, you receive the Save As dialog box, where you can determine the drive and directory to which the file will be saved.

These steps work in both Netscape and Internet Explorer.

1. open the URL: **http://www.ala.org**

    You connect to the American Library Association home page.

2. place your mouse pointer on the ALA logo

3. click the RIGHT mouse button

4. in *Netscape,* click on **Save Image As**

   OR

   in *Internet Explorer,* click on **Save Picture As**

5. in the **Save As** box, replace the default file name for the ALA logo with the name **ala**

HINT   *Windows 95/NT automatically adds the .gif extension to downloaded picture files as they are saved.*

6. select the C: drive and the **busy** folder

   Your Save As window now resembles this:

7. click on the **Save** button to save the file **ala.gif** to your C: drive

8. open the URL: **http://lcweb.loc.gov/**

   You connect to the Library of Congress home page.

9. place your mouse pointer on the Library of Congress logo

10. click the RIGHT mouse button

11. in *Netscape,* click on **Save Image As**

    OR

    in *Internet Explorer,* click on **Save Picture As**

12. in the **Save As** box, replace the default file name for the ALA logo with the name **loc**

HINT   *Windows 95/NT automatically adds the .gif extension to downloaded picture files as they are saved.*

13. select the **C:** drive and the **busy** folder

Your **Save As** window now resembles this:

14. click on the **Save** button to save the file loc.gif to your **C:** drive

> **HINT** *You will use the two .gif files you just downloaded when you create HTML pages in chapter 4.*

ABOUT FILES YOUR BROWSER CAN'T DISPLAY

When Netscape cannot show you a file after you clicked on its link, you get an Unknown File Type dialog box. If you click on the Save File button choice in this box, you can download the file you have chosen, or you can configure Netscape to view the file. When Internet Explorer cannot show you a file, it gives you a dialog box that offers you the option to save the file in question.

Web browsers have the ability to show you many different file types and can be configured to load or launch many common files, such as Microsoft PowerPoint presentations. When your browser cannot show or launch a file, it is either not configured to do so or the file is of a type that simply cannot be used through a Web browser or any other program.

Netscape 4.x offers better multimedia support than version 3.x. The 4.x utilities to support multimedia are optional, however, and you may not automatically receive them from your ISP or employer. When you click on a file that Netscape is not configured to open, you see the Unknown File Type dialog box:

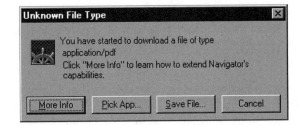

OR

The Warning dialog box:

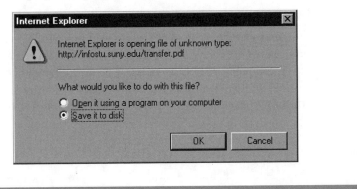

These dialog boxes are telling you that Netscape is not configured to handle the file on which you clicked and are offering you the choice of saving the file to a local disk so you can deal with it some other way.

Internet Explorer is seamlessly configured to handle a variety of sound and motion picture files. When it does encounter a file it cannot play or display, you see:

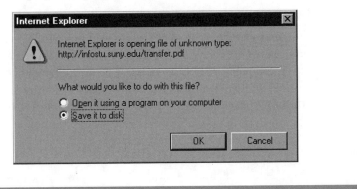

YOUR BROWSER: AN ALL-PURPOSE INTERNET INTERFACE

You can connect to almost any kind of site on the Internet through your browser. Other types of servers include Gopher (see chapter 9), FTP (see chapter 7), and Telnet (see chapter 6). You can build a URL from any kind of Internet address. For example, you are given these three types of resources:

Site	Address	URL
FTP archives at Oakland College	oak.oakland.edu	ftp://oak.oakland.edu
Library of Congress Gopher	marvel.loc.gov	gopher://marvel.loc.gov
Hofstra University Catalog via Telnet	vaxa.hofstra.edu	telnet://vaxa.hofstra.edu

What is the advantage of doing FTP, Gopher, and Telnet through Netscape? Well, FTP and Gopher sites are much easier to navigate using the point-and-click system of a graphical browser, and it's just plain convenient to be able to stay in Netscape to Telnet, especially when you encounter a Telnet link in an HTML document.

OTHER FILE FORMATS

The Web environment is characterized not only by navigation through hypertext links but also by its multimedia offerings. Information can be read, enjoyed in still or motion pictures, or heard through your computer's speakers.

Sound Files

You find sound files on Web sites as well as visual formats. Common file extensions for sound files are .au or .wav. On an IBM-compatible personal computer, you need a properly configured sound board and speakers to hear audio files (sound capability is built into Macintosh computers). Here is an example of a Web site offering links to sound files:

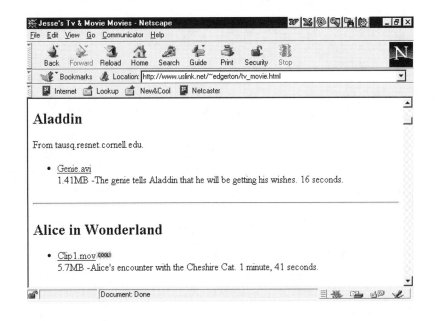

Movies   There are a variety of motion picture file types. Some of the file extensions that you encounter on the Internet are Video for Windows (.avi), QuickTime (.qt or .mov), and MPEG (.mpg or .mpeg). Motion picture files can be downloaded as easily as HTML files by using the Save As or Save As File features under your browser's File menu. This is an example of a Web site offering links to movie clips:

COLLECTING THE SKEINS OF THE WEB

The World Wide Web, or simply the Web, is the hypertext information subset of the Internet. Hypertext documents, still pictures, and sound and motion picture files can all be accessed on computers running HyperText Transport Protocol (http) software. These servers are accessed by Web browser software that runs on your local computer. The two most popular browsers are Netscape and Internet Explorer. Browsers are uniquely designed to show hypertext documents and their links to other Web resources as well as a variety of multimedia file formats.

Web browsers can also be used to access other types of Internet information formats such as FTP archives and Gopher. Uniform Resource Locators (URLs) are the addresses used to connect to all varieties of Internet servers. The scheme, or prefix, of the URL determines to what kind of server the browser points. Possible schemes are http://, ftp://, gopher://, and telnet://. The flexible nature of a browser allows you to use it as an all-purpose Internet interface.

The process of following a trail of links through a Web browser is called browsing or surfing the Internet. The World Wide Web is the fastest growing part of the Internet, and the majority of institutions and companies serving information on the Internet are using the hypertext format or converting existing formats, such as Gopher, to hypertext.

Get Hyper and Create
Your Own Web Pages

4

WHAT IS HTML?

HTML, HyperText Markup Language, is a computer language designed to send commands to a Web browser, such as Netscape, and tell it how to display text documents and other types of information.

SGML

Have you heard of SGML (Standardized General Markup Language)? Well, HTML is derived from SGML. (SGML standards fill two thick volumes.) SGML is a complex standard for electronic document formatting that attempts to make the finished product a close facsimile of the paper original. SGML can be used in a wide variety of software applications with little or no variation in their appearance, but the reader of an HTML document can change the font size, eliminate the background, and eliminate illustrations by adjusting the appearance options in a Web browser.

An HTML document is a simple ASCII text (also called Plain Text or DOS Text) file with HTML tags added to define the text in a way that is understood by all WWW browsers. These tags are ASCII characters positioned before and/or after sections of text. Some tags tell the browsers how to display the text. For example:

this text is bold

is displayed through your browser as:

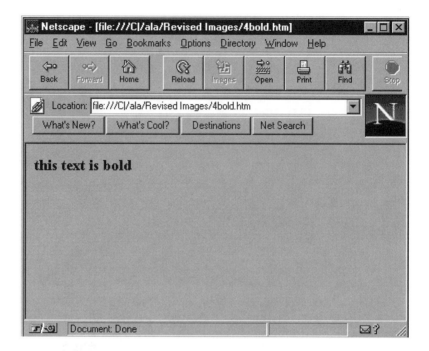

The tags are placed in angle brackets, < >; paired tags are placed at the beginning and end of the text. The first tag activates the chosen format. The format is turned off by the same tag placed at the end of the selected text but containing a forward slash, /, before the tag.

The tags themselves are not case sensitive.

A home page is the introductory document to other documents and resources on the Internet. You can think of it as the top layer in a hypertext/multimedia file stack. You will create a simple home page in an exercise later in this chapter.

WHY LEARN HTML?

Libraries are a large presence on the Internet. The typical library page offers links to the online catalog, personnel information, and ready-reference sites on the Web. If you haven't been asked to create or edit HTML pages for your library's Web site, there is a strong probability that such a request is in your near future. Even if you never have to perform hands-on editing, understanding HTML empowers you to work effectively with the individuals responsible for the actual formatting of HTML documents. Another great reason for learning HTML is that creating Web pages is fun and often artistic, and we could all use more activities with those qualities.

To create an HTML document, the bare minimum you need includes a

plan for what you want

word processor or text editor (or HTML editor)

knowledge of HTML tags

To publish your HTML documents on the Web, the bare minimum you need is storage space on a Web server in a designated directory.

To gain access to a Web server, you can save and publish your Web pages on your Internet service providers's Web server, or you may be allowed to put your Web pages on a Web server where you work. The big online services such as America Online, CompuServe, or Microsoft Network allow you to publish Web pages from your account. The procedures for saving your pages to a Web server vary from ISP to ISP, so ask for specific instructions.

LEVELS OF HTML

There are three levels of HTML formatting. At the time of publication, the current, officially approved standard is HTML 3.2, which governs tags recognized by almost all Web browsers. See Introducing HTML 3.2 at http://www.w3.org/MarkUp/Wilbur for more information.

FORMAT TAGS

Format tags control the appearance and position of text in your HTML document. Use them to modify the appearance of your text as you would using word processing software.

Relative Type Styles

You can choose the relative size and styles of characters in your text file using format tags. The type styles produced by the following tags are relative because they are determined by the individual browser. Headings appear bigger and bolder than other text. Heading 1 is the largest and most prominent, and each subsequent heading is smaller. The contents of the heading tag determine type size.

`<h1>. . .</h1>`	# Heading 1
`<h2>. . .</h2>`	## Heading 2
`<h3>. . .</h3>`	### Heading 3
`<h4>. . .</h4>`	#### Heading 4
`<h5>. . .</h5>`	##### Heading 5
`<h6>. . .</h6>`	###### Heading 6

The title tag places text in the title bar of the document window when it is opened in a Web browser such as Netscape or Internet Explorer.

`<title>. . . </title>`

Other relative type style tags are

`<strong> . . . </strong>`	usually **bold** or *italic*
`<em> . . . </em>`	emphasizes text with **bold** or *italics*
`<kbd> . . . </kbd>`	presents text in a fixed pitch `Courier font`

Fixed Type Styles

Styles that are fixed will appear the same way in all graphical browsers.

`<I> . . . </I>`	*italics*
`<b> . . . </b>`	**bold**
`<u> . . . </u>`	<u>underline</u>

HINT *As in the above example, the letters used in the HTML tags may be either upper or lowercase.*

ADDITIONAL TAGS

The following tags are essential to every HTML document. Use them to add blank lines, break lines, and define the sections of your document.

`<p>`	the tag for the end of a paragraph forces a line break followed by a blank line
` `	breaks a line in a specific place; lines that do not end with this tag will adjust to the various window sizes selected in a browser
`<html>`	the first tag in your document signals the beginning of an HTML document
`</html>`	the last tag in your document

There are two parts to every document:

<head> . . . </head>   designates the document's title

<body> . . . </body>   designates the body of the document

TEXT LINKS

Of course you want your document to do more than just look good. You want it to be hyper(text). You can make an active link to another file on your server or a remote WWW server by inserting a link tag that looks like this:

<a href="filename.html"> . . . </a>

<a href="http://wwwserver.domain/directory/filename"> . . . </a>

GRAPHICS FILES

There is one graphics file type that all graphical Web browsers can display. The type is Graphic Interchange Format and the file extension is .gif. You can find ready-made .gif files in many locations all over the Internet. (Connect to http://www.iconbazaar.com for one of the best collections.) To create .gif files you can scan pictures or drawings and edit them in graphic art software such as Adobe Photoshop or convert a format such as .BMP (Window's Paint Brush) to .gif using conversion software. You can also buy .gif files from computer software vendors. Before publishing any graphics files on the web, be *sure* that they are in the public domain. (When in doubt, ask for permission to reproduce a graphic.)

The current rule of thumb is to keep your graphics file size to 40 Kbps or less. Based on the calculation that a 28.8 Kbps modem transfers a file at 2 KB, 20 seconds is a reasonable time to wait for graphics to load.

Jpeg files are another graphics file type. They have an extension of .jpg or .jpe and can be read by all graphical Web browsers.

You can add an image file to illustrate your HTML document using the image source tag. Graphics files can be located locally on your Web server or remotely on someone else's. The tag to link to a remote graphic is composed like this:

<img src="http://host.subdomain.domain/path/filename.gif">

The tag to add a locally stored graphic is composed as follows:

<img src="filename.gif">

You can align a graphic with text using the align attribute within the img src (image source) tag. These are your align attribute choices:

<img align=top src="file.gif">	Puts text at the top of a graphic
<img align=middle src="file.gif">	Puts text at the middle of a graphic
<img align=bottom src="file.gif">	Puts text at the bottom of a graphic

Text Alternatives to Graphics

Not everyone has a graphical browser, or some people set their Web browser so it does not automatically load images, therefore decreasing the amount of time it takes pages to load. You can enter a text alternative to a graphic by adding the alt= command to your image source tag. For example:

alt="[this is a picture]"

DIVIDING RULES

Horizontal lines are an excellent way to visually divide and organize a document. Whenever you wish to insert a line into an HTML document, you simply add the <hr> tag.

E-MAIL LINKS

You can establish links to sites that are not Web sites. Sites that do not serve hypertext information will have URLs that begin with ftp://, or telnet://, or gopher:// (See chapter 3 for more information about URLs.) You can also create a link that will allow someone to activate the mail program contained in his or her browser (such as Netscape Mail) and send a message to a designated e-mail address. An e-mail link looks like this:

<a href="mailto: yourname@yourdomain.com">Click here to send me mail.</a>

You can add an e-mail link to your document by typing the above tag and replacing yourname@yourdomain.com with your own e-mail address.

LISTS (A QUICK LOOK)

Once you get comfortable with formatting and linking tags you will want to try your hand at lists and forms. Forms are addressed in more advanced and comprehensive Internet publications. These are list tags:

\<ol> . . . \</ol>	ordered (numbered) lists
\<ul> . . . \</ul>	unnumbered bulleted lists
\<li>	list item

ANCHOR AND NAME TAGS

You can assign a name tag to selected portions of text within your document and then set up an active link in another part of the document that points to the name tag. In the following exercise you will assign the name tag *top* to the first line of the document. This name tag is called the *anchor*.

STARTING YOUR OWN HOME PAGE

One of the best ways to learn HTML tags is to create a page without the assistance of an HTML editor. In the following exercise you create a simple home page using Windows Notepad (look under Start, Programs, Accessories).

After you create this page by typing in every tag, you can try out the next exercise and create a page using an HTML editor.

1. open Windows Notepad

   You have a blank document in front of you.

2. type in the following text to begin your home page

   \<html>

   \<head>\<title>My Home Page.\</title>

   \</head>

<body>

<p>

<h1>Hello, my name is_[put your name here]**.</h1>**

<p>

<i>There are so many interesting things to do on the Internet!</i>

<p>

<h2>Below are some interesting Internet sites I have chosen for my home page.</h2>

<p>

I am making a bold statement here.

<p>

3. type in the remote link tags like this:

<a href="http://www.yahoo.com">Click here for Yahoo.</a>

<p>

<a href="http://webcrawler.com/">Click here for WebCrawler</a>

<p>

HINT   *This is a good place to save your file.*

4. click on **File** in the menu bar

5. click on **Save**

6. select the **filename box** and type **homepage.htm** as your filename

7. select the **C:** drive and the **busy** folder/directory as your destination (See Making an Exercise Directory for information on creating your **busy** folder.)

8. you can now periodically save by choosing **File**, then **Save**

HINT   *When you want to open your homepage.htm document in Notepad, you'll need to change the Files of type: to All Files [*.*] to see the homepage.htm file name because it doesn't have a .txt extension.*

In chapter 3 you downloaded to your *busy* folder on the C: drive the ALA masthead as ala.gif and the Library of Congress logo as loc.gif. It is saved on your disk as loc.gif. (If you did not perform this download exercise, please do so now.) You will now add these two images to your page.

9. type the image source tag into your document now:

   <img src="ala.gif">

   <p>

HINT *You can make a graphic be a link to another file by combining the two types of tags.*

You will now make the above graphic be a link to the ALA site.

10. to combine the tags, type the <a href . . . > </a> tags around the image tag

    <a href="http://www.ala.org"><img src="ala.gif">**</a>**

HINT *When a user clicks on the picture produced by the graphic, he or she links to the ALA Web search site.*

You should add some instructions regarding the need to click on the graphic picture to make the link to the file. These instructions can be typed as plain text on the same line as the file link and image source tags or be part of the link. You will make the instructions part of the link by inserting them before the </a> tag which ends the <a href="http://www.ala.org"> tag.

11. type this sentence now, on the same line as the combined tags, *before* the **</a>** tag:

    Click on the picture to connect to the ALA home page.

    <p>

12. type the following lines now:

    <a href="http://www.loc.gov"><img align=TOP src="loc.gif">Click here for the Library of Congress</a>

    <p>

    The Library of Congress has an extensive Web site.

    <p>

13. insert a text alternative to your Library of Congress logo by inserting the bolded text below to your existing tag information (this aids users of a text-only browser, or users browsing without images loading):

    <a href="http://www.loc.gov"><img align=TOP src="loc.gif" **alt="[Library of Congress logo]**">Click here for the Library of Congress</a> The Library of Congress has an extensive Web site.

    <p>

14. type in the horizontal rule tag now (it places a line across your page):

    <hr>

15. type these two short lists into your document now:

    <p>

    HTML Tips:

    <ol>

    <li>Plunge in and create a Home Page.

    <li>Refine the Home Page after creating it, before publicizing it.

    <li>Don't use big graphics.

    </ol>

    <p>

    HTML Goals List:

    <ul>

    <li>Make your documents short, clean, and readable.

    <li>Reach your intended audience.

    <li>Keep your Web site up to date.

    </ul>

16. move your cursor to the first line of your homepage.htm practice document and after the <html> tag insert the name tags around your title as follows (type in only the bold tags, the other information should already be there):

    <a name="top"><head><title>My Home Page</title>**</a>**

    <p>

> **HINT**   *The first code, <a name="top">, identifies the start of the text named* top, *and the second code, </a>, identifies its end. (Note that the <head> <title> tags are contained within the <a name=> tag.)*

    Now you can return to the bottom of your first HTML document.

17. type in an active link that points to the named text, or anchor, called *top*:

    <a href="#top">Click here to return to the top of the document.</a>

    <p>

18. type these two tags now to tag the end of the body of your home page

    </body>

    </html>

TEST DRIVE YOUR HOME PAGE IN A BROWSER

It is time to take your first home page HTML document for a spin by looking at it through your Netscape or Internet Explorer graphical browser.

EXERCISE

1. pull down the Notepad **File** menu
2. choose **Save**

HINT   *Notepad saves your document as plain ASCII text, thereby allowing it to be read by your browser. If you create your HTML document with word processing software, you must use the Save as type list box and select the option Plain Text or ASCII text.*
You don't have to have a WWW server to be able to load your own HTML files; you can open them like any other file your browser finds on the Web.

3. leave **Notepad** active
4. open Netscape or Internet Explorer
5. in the *Netscape* menu bar, click on **File** and click on **Open Page** (or **Open File**)

   OR

   in the *Internet Explorer* menu bar, click on **File** and click on **Open**
6. in the dialog box provided, type **c:\busy\homepage.htm**
7. click **OK**

   You should see your new home page in all its glory.
8. check to make sure that all links are working properly

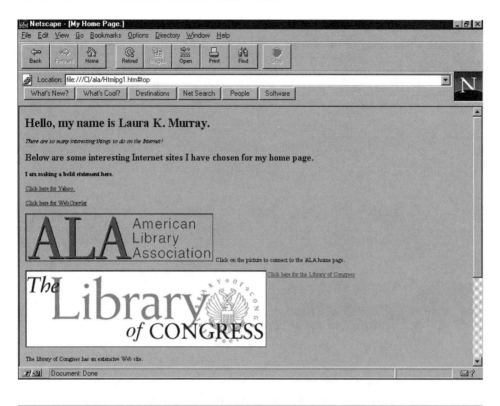

HTML Tips:

1. Plunge in and create a Home Page.
2. Refine the Home Page after creating it, before publicizing it.
3. Don't use big graphics.

HTML Goals List:

* Make your documents short, clean and readable.
* Reach your intended audience.
* Keep your Web site up to date.

Click here to return to the top of the document.

HINT *If you find an error in your home page, you can check your HTML by clicking on View in the menu bar. In Netscape then click on Document Source or Page Source. In Internet Explorer click on View, then Source. (Source allows you to see the actual HTML document or source.) In Netscape, you can check your tags, but you cannot edit them. In Internet Explorer you are actually viewing the source in Notepad; therefore, you can edit it, but you are unable to save over your original file.*

If you wish to make corrections now, follow these steps:

9. switch back to Notepad

10. make the corrections you desire

11. save the document again

12. switch back to your Netscape or Internet Explorer browser

13. in *Netscape,* click on the **Reload** button to reload the document with its corrections

    OR

    in *Internet Explorer,* click on **Refresh**

HTML EDITORS

The most-recent versions of popular word processing software allow you to convert documents to the HTML format. Netscape Communicator also allows you to perform HTML editing with its Composer application (see the next section). Sophisticated, easy-to-use stand-alone HTML editors are also available. (It is good to know how to do it manually, as you learned in steps 9–13, so you understand how these programs work.)

HTML editors work much the same as word processors except that they allow you to add hyper links and other elements specific to HTML. Using an editor allows you to create attractive and accurate pages quickly. Many editors offer spell checking as well as checkers for your tags that locate errors and improper syntax. You'll probably find that you prefer creating pages in editors but will perform minor editing manually with a handy text editor like Notepad.

Netscape Composer

Composer is the HTML editor that comes with the Netscape Communicator suite of applications. The entire Communicator suite can be downloaded from the Netscape home page at http://www.netscape.com.

 Composer can be found in the Netscape Communicator folder (or opened through the Netscape File menu). Look for Page Composer in the menu selection.

1. start **Netscape Composer**

   You see a screen like this:

2. note how the buttons on the top toolbar are labeled

3. point to each button on the **Formatting** toolbar

HINT *The formatting toolbar is the lower one, and the Windows bubble help tells you what each button is for.*

For this exercise you'll need these buttons:

   Link
   Image
   Table
   Bold
   Numbered List
   Increase Indent

You'll also need these pull-down menus:

   File
   View
   Format

Composer is a **WYSIWYG** *editor. WYSIWYG (pronounced wizie wig) is the acronym for what you see is what you get. Instead of showing you the HTML tags, Composer shows you how your document will look when it is opened in a browser. You* are *able to see the HTML tags if you need to (see Behind the Scenes in Composer on page 55). The Composer* **Help** *feature provides step-by-step instructions for using Composer and should be reviewed carefully.*

You can get a jump start using Composer by creating another Web page.

4. click on the **New** dog-eared icon

5. on the **Create New Page** menu, which appears next, click on **Blank Page**

6. type: **My Second Page**

7. press the **ENTER** key

8. click on **File**, then **Save**

9. select the **busy** folder on the C: drive as your **Save in** location

10. in the **File name** box type **page2.htm**

Your **Save As** dialog box looks like this:

11. click on the **Save** button

You are asked for a title; the information you enter here appears in the title bar of your document.

12. type: **My Second Page**

13. click **OK**

You are now looking at the first sentence of your second home page.

14. select the text you have already typed (**My Second Page**)

15. click on the **Format** menu, then **Headings**, then **1**

    The text should now be displayed in the biggest heading style.

16. make sure My Second Page isn't highlighted, and press the **ENTER** key

17. now type: **Greetings. This is my second Web page created with Netscape Composer. Here are some good library-related sites:**

18. press the **ENTER** key twice

19. click on the **Link** button

20. in the **Enter text to display for a new link** box, type: **Click here for the Library of Congress**

21. in the **Link to a page location or local file** box, type: **http://libweb.loc.gov**

22. click **OK**; you should now see: **Click here for the Library of Congress**

    This is your first hyperlink in Composer.

23. press the **ENTER** key to go to a new line

24. click on the **Image** button

25. in the **Image location** box, type in the file name for the Library of Congress .gif file you downloaded earlier: **loc.gif**

26. click **OK**

27. click on the **paragraph** button to insert a blank line

    You should now see the Library of Congress logo.

    So far, your second page looks something like this:

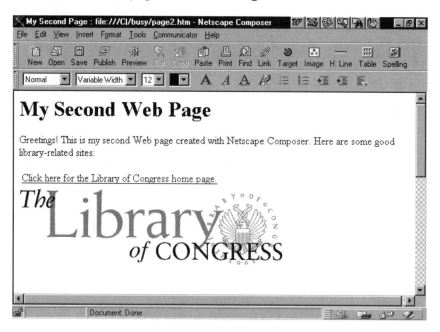

28. click on the **paragraph** button to insert a blank line

29. click on the **Link** button

30. in the **Enter text to display for a new link** box, type: **Click here for the American Library Association home page**

31. in the **Link to a page location or local file** box, type: **http://www.ala.org**

32. click **OK**; you should now see: <u>**Click here for the American Library Association home page**</u>

33. click on the **Image** button

34. in the **Image location** box, type in the file name for the American Library Association .gif file you downloaded earlier: **ala.gif**

35. click **OK**

You now see the American Library Association logo.

BEHIND THE SCENES IN COMPOSER

Now is a good time to take a peek behind the scenes at the HTML tags that Composer secretly inserts into your document.

1. click on **View**

2. click on **Page Source**

Look at all the tags that you did not have to type:

```
Netscape
<HTML>
<HEAD>
    <META HTTP-EQUIV="Content-Type" CONTENT="text/html; charset=iso-8859-1">
    <META NAME="Author" CONTENT="lkm">
    <META NAME="GENERATOR" CONTENT="Mozilla/4.01 [en] (Win95; I) [Netscape]">
    <TITLE>My Second Page</TITLE>
</HEAD>
<BODY>

<H1>
My Second Web Page</H1>
Greetings! This is my second Web page created with Netscape Composer. Here
are some good library-related sites:

<P> <A HREF="http://www.loc.gov">Click here for the Library of Congress
home page.</A>
<BR><IMG SRC="loc.gif" HEIGHT=125 WIDTH=413>

<P> 
<BR>  <A HREF="http://www.ala.org">Click here for the American Library
Association home page.</A>
<BR><IMG SRC="ala.gif" HEIGHT=77 WIDTH=322>
<BR> 
<BR> 
<BR> 
```

36. close the **Page Source** window

37. press the **ENTER** key after the ALA graphic to insert a blank line

38. type: **My goals for this page:**

39. press the **ENTER** key again

40. click on the **Numbered List** button on the toolbar (it has 123 on it)

41. a # sign appears

42. next to the # sign type: **Set up a table**

43. press the **ENTER** key

44. next to the new # sign type: **Indent text**

45. press the **ENTER** key

46. click on the **Numbered List** button again to end your list

47. now type: **This is my first table:**

48. press the **ENTER** key

49. click on the **Table** button (it looks like a waffle)

    You should see the **New Table Properties** dialog box:

50. set the number of rows to **3** in the text box provided

51. set the number of columns to **3**

52. find and click on the **OK** button at the bottom of the **New Table Properties** box

   The borders of an empty table will appear with your cursor blinking in the first cell.

> **HINT** *You can enter information into the table by tabbing between cells or pointing to each cell and clicking to insert a cursor. You can format the text within a table cell* and *put image and document links into a table.*

53. select the text within the top row of cells and click on the **Bold** button (it has a bold capital letter **A** on it)

   Your table may look like this:

```
My Second Page : file:///C|/busy/page2.htm - Netscape Composer        _ □ ×
File  Edit  View  Insert  Format  Tools  Communicator  Help

 New  Open  Save  Publish  Preview   Cut  Copy  Paste  Print  Find  Link  Target  Image  H. Line  Table  Spelling

 Normal  ▼  Variable Width ▼  12 ▼  ■ ▼   A  A  A  𝒜  ⋮≡  ≣  ⬌  ⬌  ☰

My Goals for this Page:

    #  Set up a table
    #  Indent text

This is my first table:|

 ┌─────────────────┬─────────────────┬─────────────────┐
 │ Column 1        │ Column 2        │ Column 3        │
 ├─────────────────┼─────────────────┼─────────────────┤
 │ data item       │ data item       │ data item       │
 ├─────────────────┼─────────────────┼─────────────────┤
 │ data item       │ data item       │ data item       │
 └─────────────────┴─────────────────┴─────────────────┘


 Start  Personal Hom...  compose5 - P...  Exploring - ala...  My Secon...          9:51 AM
```

54. type the following sentences into your document (substitute your own words if you wish):

   The profession of library science is in a continual upheaval due to rapidly changing computer technologies. As soon as an information professional masters the use of a particular software he or she finds that a new version is released, and the learning process begins again.

55. select the text you just typed

 HINT   *Click and drag to select.*

56. click on the **Increase Indent** button (the arrow points right toward lines on it)

Now your paragraph is indented.

57. click on the **Increase Indent** button again to indent further

58. click on **Save** again

Voilà! You now have a second HTML page. You can preview it by clicking on the **Preview** button, then edit it again if you find any mistakes.

Netscape Composer has many features that cannot be covered in this quick guide. By now you are probably comfortable enough to explore additional menus and buttons on your own. Use the Help feature if you get stumped.

PUBLISHING YOUR PAGES

There is no one way to copy your pages to a Web server and make them accessible on the Web. It is best to consult your Web server administrator, or Webmaster, as to appropriate procedure for loading your Web pages.

A HYPER LOOK BACK

Learning HTML is as easy as learning word processing. It is more gratifying, however, because you create dynamic multimedia documents that are published in an international forum and are accessible to millions of people. Your library community can expand by millions through the power of a home page on the World Wide Web.

You will find that your vocabulary of HTML tags grows with use. This chapter taught you the basic tags that allow you to create coherent Web pages. As your command of HTML increases, your pages become more communicative, and you become less of a foreigner in the culture of the Web.

Where and How to Learn More

Learning HTML is very much like learning a foreign language. You now know enough to communicate simply and coherently in the Web subculture. You can now build your tag vocabulary through other resources such as the following Web sites and books.

The Bare Bones Guide to HTML

http://werbach.com/barebones/barebone.html

> "The Guide lists all the tags that current versions of most browsers are likely to recognize. [It] is designed to be as concise as possible."

The NCSA Beginners' Guide to HTML

http://www.ncsa.uiuc.edu/General/Internet/WWW/HTMLPrimer.html

> "The guide is used by many to start to understand the hypertext markup language (HTML) used on the World Wide Web. It is an introduction and does not pretend to offer instructions on every aspect of HTML."

Lemay, Laura. *Teach Yourself Web Publishing with HTML 3.2 in 14 Days, the Professional Reference Edition*. Indianapolis, Ind.: Macmillan, 1997.

> "Anyone can learn HTML and Web publishing. This easy-to-read, easy-to-understand book carefully steps you through everything you'll need to know—from the fundamentals of creating a simple home page to the intricacies of designing and creating elaborate Web sites with advanced HTML, CGI scripts, and JavaScript and Java programs." Order through http://slack.lne.com/Web/.

Metz, Ray E., and Gail Junion-Metz. *Using the World Wide Web and Creating Home Pages*. New York: Neal-Schuman, 1996.

> "Like other books in Neal-Schuman's How To and Net-Guide series, *Using the World Wide Web and Creating Home Pages* is designed for library administrators, professional and support staff, and interested patrons."

CHAPTER 5

Global Communication Choices: Listserv, E-Mail, UseNet, and Chat

You can send and receive electronic mail messages via the Internet using your local e-mail program and Internet access. Numerous conferences or discussion groups on various topics allow you to receive and send e-mail in your areas of interest.

ELECTRONIC CONFERENCES

An electronic conference is a forum for discussing a specific topic via e-mail. Electronic conferences are also called "discussion lists" or "mailing lists." Someone organizes a conference by setting up a program to manage the conference messages on a computer that is accessible via the Internet. The conference is then announced in print and electronic form so that Internet participants will know how to subscribe to it.

Subscribers to an electronic conference receive e-mail messages posted by other subscribers or by the conference owners and moderators. Subscribers may then respond to these postings or contribute messages of their own. Many interesting and useful discussions take place in these conferences.

The most common mailing-list management software program is called Listserv. Listserv is so popular that electronic conferences are often generically called "listservs." You may come across other less-popular e-mail software programs such as List-Proc and Majordomo, but this chapter concentrates on Listserv.

How to Subscribe to an Electronic Conference

To subscribe to a listserv, obtain the e-mail address and subscription commands for the conference. You find lists of e-conferences in Internet books, periodicals, and directories on the Web. A comprehensive compilation of library-related e-mail discussion lists is found at http://www.netstrider.com/library/listservs/.

Electronic conferences have two e-mail addresses: one to which you send commands (such as subscribing and unsubscribing) and one to which you send actual contributions or postings. If the list is managed by Listserv software, the address to which you send commands has the form LISTSERV@ADDRESS. The address to which you send messages has the form CONFERENCE-NAME@ADDRESS. (If the list is managed by Majordomo software, the address to which you send commands has the form MAJORDOMO@ADDRESS.)

Send your subscription request to the correct address. Then look for an e-mail message acknowledging your subscription or asking for a confirmation response. Save any introductory messages containing instructions and guidelines for future reference. For example:

Conference name:	PACS-L (Public Access Computer Systems Forum)
Address for commands:	LISTSERV@UHUPVM1.UH.EDU
Message to send:	subscribe pacs-l YourFirstName YourLastName
Address for postings:	PACS-L@UHUPVM1.UH.EDU (do not send subscription requests to this address)

Overview of Basic Listserv Commands

You join a listserv e-mail list by sending the *subscribe* command to the listserv address. If you don't like the list, you can *unsubscribe*. When you take a vacation and don't want the messages from a listserv to pile up in your mailbox, you can send the *nomail* command to temporarily suspend your receipt of messages. Your receipt of messages is resumed when you send the *mail* command.

subscribe list-name	To join the discussion forum
unsubscribe list-name	To sign off (or unsubscribe) from the discussion forum
set list-name nomail	Useful if you're going on vacation and don't want to unsubscribe from the list; the NOMAIL option tells the listserver not to send mail to your address
set list-name mail	To begin receiving mail again (undoes the NOMAIL option)

MANAGING E-MAIL THROUGH YOUR BROWSER

To use the mail features of your browser, you need to tell it where your mail servers are. If you are using an Internet connection at work, your local support people may have done this for you.

If you receive an error message about mail servers after trying to start your mail program, then follow these instructions to configure your browser. Netscape is covered first, then Internet Explorer.

There are two types of protocols for sending mail on the Internet:

SMTP   Simple Mail Transfer Protocol
POP   Post Office Protocol

SMTP is part of the TCP/IP suite of protocols. Its purpose is to carry the flow of e-mail messages to and from servers on the Internet. POP controls the storage and retrieval of e-mail messages, as does a traditional U.S. mail post office. While there are a variety of e-mail softwares to use for Internet mail, they are all compliant with SMTP and POP.

Obtain the following information from your ISP:

1. Your complete Internet e-mail address (usually youraccountname@mailserver.address.domain)

2. The address of your ISP's POP mail server

3. The address of your ISP's SMTP server

Setting Up Your Mail Servers in Netscape

For Navigator 4.x

1. click on **Edit**

2. click on **Preferences**

3. click on **Mail Server**

4. click on **Mail & Groups**

5. enter your account **I.D.**

6. enter your outgoing mail and incoming mail information

For example:

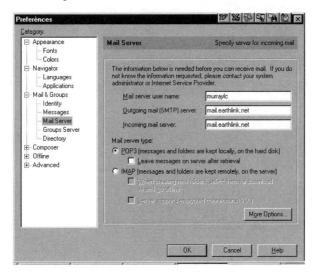

7. click **OK**

For Netscape 3.x

1. click on **Options**

2. click on **Mail and News Preferences**

3. click on **Servers**

4. enter the server information

Your window resembles this:

Now you are ready to actually use Netscape Mail!

Using Netscape Mail to Subscribe to an Electronic Conference

In this exercise you subscribe to PACS-L using Netscape Navigator.

EXERCISE
---

1. start **Netscape Navigator**
2. click on the **mailbox** icon in the lower right corner of the Navigator window

> **HINT** *The mailbox icon may be an envelope or it may be envelopes with a mail bin.*

3. if asked for the password for your ISP account, enter your Password
4. click **OK**

5. click on the **To:** or **New Message** button to begin creating a new message

   If your cursor is not flashing at the **To:** prompt, click on the **Address** button to get one.

6. enter the address: **listserv@uhupvm1.uh.edu**
7. skip the **Subject:** text box

HINT *Leave the subject line blank only when subscribing to a listserv e-mail list.*

8. click in the **message** text box

9. type: **subscribe PACS-L** *yourfirstname yourlastname*

Your window resembles this:

```
Composition                                                    _ □ ×
File  Edit  View  Insert  Format  Tools  Communicator  Help

  Send   Quote  Address  Attach  Spelling  Save  Security  Stop     N

    To:  LISTSERV@UHUPVM1.UH.EDU



Subject:

Normal  Variable Width  12    A A A A ...

subscribe pacs-l laura k. murray



              Document: Done
```

10. click on the **send** button

HINT *If you are prompted for a subject after clicking send, just click OK.*

Composing a Netscape Mail Message

The following is an *example* rather than an actual hands-on exercise. You can use it to guide you through creating and sending your own mail message and attachment to an acquaintance through Netscape.

In this example, a new message and an attached file (the text of *White Fang*, by Jack London) is composed in Netscape Mail and sent to an individual.

EXERCISE

1. start **Netscape Mail**

2. click on **New Message**

3. enter the recipient's address in the **To:** line, for example:

   myfriend@server.isp.com

4. enter a subject, for example:

   Hi from your friend!

5. enter the text of a message, for example:

   Hi friend, here is the full text of Jack London's *White Fang.* Happy reading!

6. click on the **Attach** button

HINT   *You can attach any kind of file or a Web page (such as the one you created in chapter 4) to a mail message.*

7. locate the file you wish to attach, for example:

   locate the **wtfng.txt** file on the **C:** drive in the **busy** directory

HINT   *The **wtfng.txt** file mentioned in the example is downloaded using FTP as described in chapter 7.*

8. click on **Open**

   You see the final Composition window with the path and file name of the attached file:

9. click on **Send** to send your completed message

MANAGING NETSCAPE MAIL

When you join a mailing list or start a regular correspondence based on e-mail, you'll receive new e-mail messages daily. You'll need to know how to handle them efficiently.

When you first start Netscape Mail, your window looks like this:

Using Netscape Mail is pretty straightforward.

Activity	Action
Reading a message you receive	double-click on the message
Copying a message from the remote mail server to your local drive	click on the **Get Msg** button
Replying to a message	click on the message to select it, or double-click on it to read it click on the **Reply** button
Forwarding a message	click on the message to select it, or double-click on it to read it click on the **Forward** button

Creating a mail folder

click on **File, New Folder**
type in the name for a new folder
   (The default placement for the new
   folder is to be a subfolder of your
   Inbox folder and will look like this:)

New Folder

Name:	personal
Create as sub-folder of:	Inbox

OK

Cancel

Saving a message to a
  particular folder

click on the message to select it, or
  double-click on it to read it
click on the **File** icon button
click on the folder to which you wish
  to move the file

Retrieving a message
  from a folder other
  than the Inbox

click on the listbox of folder names
  (The default folder is probably
  Inbox, which looks like this:)

Inbox - Netscape Folder

File Edit View Go Message Communicator Help

Get Msg New Msg Reply Forward File Next Print Sec

Inbox   ssages: 0   Unread messages: 0

Date   Priority

Local Mail
  Inbox
    personal
  Unsent Messages
  Drafts
  Sent
  Trash
  Samples
news

Document: Done

click on the folder you wish to open

Any other questions? If so, click on **Help!**

CONFIGURING SERVERS IN INTERNET EXPLORER'S INTERNET MAIL

Your server may already be configured for you. You only need to configure your server if an error message indicates it.

1. start Internet Explorer

2. click on **File** (or the letter icon)

3. click on **New Message**

   You should have activated the Internet Mail Configuration Wizard

4. click on **Next**

5. enter your **name** and **e-mail address**

6. click on **Next**

7. enter the addresses of your **Incoming** and **Outgoing** mail servers

HINT *You obtain these addresses from your ISP.*

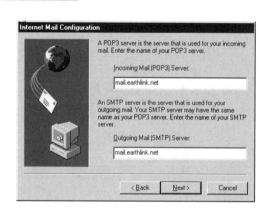

8. click on **Next**

9. enter your **e-mail account** (the account name assigned by
your ISP) and your account **password**

10. click on **Next**

11. set your type of connection

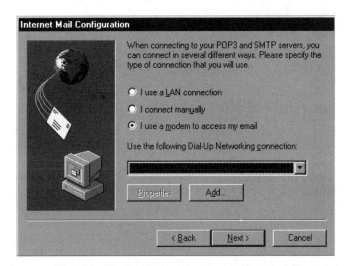

12. click on **Next**

You should get confirmation that your Wizard setup is
done and move right into your New Message window.

SUBSCRIBING TO AN E-CONFERENCE
IN INTERNET EXPLORER'S INTERNET MAIL

In this exercise you subscribe to PACS-L using Internet Explorer. Don't subscribe to PACS-L again if you already did it through Netscape. Try subscribing to another e-mail list if you want to practice through Internet Explorer.

If you are not already in the New Message window of Internet Mail:

1. start **Internet Explorer**

2. click on the **File** menu heading

3. click on **New Message**

Now you are in the New Message window:

New Message	_ □ ×
File Edit View Mail Insert Format Help	

To: []

Cc: < click here to enter carbon copy recipients >

Subject: < click here to enter the subject >

/ordPerfect...   mail20 - Paint   Internet Start...   Browse for Folder   New Mess...   2:20 P

4. at the **To:** prompt, type: **listserv@uhupvm1.uh.edu**

5. leave the **Subject** blank

HINT	*Leave the subject line blank only when subscribing to a listserv e-mail list.*

6. click in the blank **message** text box

7. type: **subscribe PACS-L yourfirstname yourlastname**

```
New Message                                                    _ □ ✕
File  Edit  View  Mail  Insert  Format  Help

  To:  LISTSERV@UHUPVM1.UH.EDU                                     🏛
  Cc:  < click here to enter carbon copy recipients >
Subject:  < click here to enter the subject >

  subscribe pacs-l laura k. murray




WordPerfect...  mail21 - Paint   Internet Start...  Browse for Folder  New Mess...  2:22 P
```

8. click on **Send** to send your completed message

Composing a Message in Internet Explorer's Internet Mail

This is an *example* rather than an actual hands-on exercise. You can use it to guide you through creating and sending your own mail message and attachment to an acquaintance through Internet Explorer's Internet Mail.

In this example, a new message and an attached file (the text of *White Fang*, by Jack London) is composed in Internet Mail and sent to an individual.

1. start **Internet Explorer**

2. click on **File**

3. click on **New Message**

4. at the **To:** prompt, type the recipient's e-mail address, for example:

myfriend@server.isp.com

5. enter a subject, for example:

Hi from your friend!

6. enter the text of a message, for example:

Hi friend, here is the full text containing Jack London's *White Fang*. Happy reading!

7. click on the **Insert** file menu heading

8. click on **File**

9. locate the file you wish to attach, for example:

locate the **wtfng.txt** file on the **C:** drive in the **busy** directory

HINT   *The **wtfng.txt** file in the example is downloaded using FTP as described in chapter 7.*

10. click on the **Attach** button

Your completed message, with attachment, looks something like this:

11. now click on the **Send** button to send your message (The Send button has a flying or stationary envelope on it.)

MANAGING INTERNET EXPLORER'S INTERNET MAIL

To start Internet Explorer, click on the **Mail** button in the Explorer toolbar, then click on **Read Mail**.

Activity	Action
Reading a message you receive	double-click on the message
Copying a message from the remote mail server to your local drive	click on the **Send and Receive** button

Replying to a message	click on the message to select it, or double-click on it to read it click on the **Reply to Author** OR the **Reply to All** button
Forwarding a message	click on the message to select it, or double-click on it to read it click on the **Forward** button
Creating a mail folder	click on **File** click on **Folder** click on **Create** type in the name for a new folder click **OK**
Moving a message to a particular folder (must be reading the message to be able to move it)	double-click on the message to read it click on the **Mail** menu heading click on the **Move To** choice click on the folder to which you wish to move the message
Retrieving a message from a folder other than the Inbox	click on the listbox of folder names click on the folder you wish to open

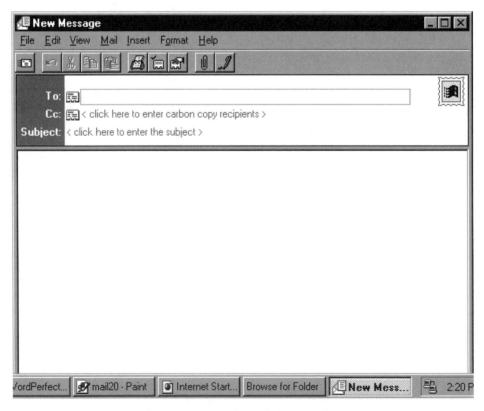

Any other questions? If so, click on **Help!**

E-MAIL ETIQUETTE (A.K.A. NETIQUETTE)

Because the Internet allows extensive typed discussions between individuals, an e-mail etiquette, or "netiquette," has been established. Don't be deceived by its quaint name. Netiquette is a necessity for survival in the e-mail subculture. Observing the rules can mean the difference between acceptance and rejection by others already functioning proficiently in the society of e-mail communication. If you follow the simple guidelines presented in the following sections, no one will suspect you are an e-mail neophyte.

Use the correct address

Never forget that there are two addresses for every e-conference. One address is for commands such as subscribe, unsubscribe, set nomail, etc. The other is for postings such as "Does anyone want to discuss techniques for managing Internet access in libraries?" The address to which you send commands is usually listserv@address or listname-request@address; the address to which you send postings is always conference-name@address. Your fellow subscribers are grateful when you do not clutter their mailboxes with messages such as "unsubscribe conference-name John Doe."

Use your respond command responsibly

Most e-mail programs allow you to respond to a message; respond allows you to retain the address from which the message was sent without retyping it. *Remember* that e-conference messages are mailed to the computer that maintains the list and not to the individual who made the original posting. Therefore, when you respond to an e-conference message, you are posting that response to the entire list. If your reply is appropriate only for the individual who posted the message to the list, create a new message in your e-mail software. Make sure you use the individual's address, not the e-conference's. This rule keeps replies such as "Hi Jane, I agree with your posting, but I'll bet the long-winded subscribers to this conference are going to deluge you with criticisms" from the eyes of the long-winded subscribers!

Make sure sarcasm or jokes are clearly identified as such so they are not misunderstood. You can use the "sideways face" conventions that follow or simply use labels such as (joke) or (sarcasm):

:-) = humor   ;-) = wink   :-(= mad or sad

Do not use boldface, italics, or underlines

They don't transmit well. Use uppercase for necessary emphasis, but don't use all uppercase because it is the Internet equivalent of shouting.

Avoid excessive punctuation

It clutters the screen.

Keep your line length at 60 characters or less

Almost any computer monitor or terminal can display this line length. If you squeeze more than 60 characters on each line of your message, you run the risk of the lines wrapping too soon by the time another receives them. Your message will appear choppy and hard to read. For example:

```
I am a librarian at a large metropolitan library. We have
an ongoing
problem with users spending hours and hours at our public
workstations
with Internet access. Time limits and sign-up sheets are
posted now,
but enforcing both the time limit and use of the sign-up
sheets has
become the most dreaded task for library employees.
```

Never send a message you would not want the whole world to read

E-mail can become public information, even when you are sending a message to a single individual. Never write things that would jeopardize your job security, relationships, or personal security if read by someone other than the intended recipient.

Make flames judiciously

Flames are outpourings of frustration or indignation via the e-mail vehicle. Flames can be directed at people or things. They *can* be eloquent, pithy, and succinct, but they are usually nasty and long-winded. Sleep on a flame before you post it. Ask yourself if you would say the words to another's face. Think about how the recipient(s) of the flame will feel. Be aware that you will receive flames in return.

USENET NEWS

UseNet news offers another form of electronic conferencing, like e-mail discussion lists. UseNet is a forum for Internet users to share information and conduct discussions via messages managed through newsreader software. UseNet is a network of computers all over the world that manages the flow of messages composing UseNet "news." You access

UseNet via a host computer that subscribes to newsgroups. Your local systems manager or Internet service provider should know if your host computer is a UseNet feed site and to what newsgroups it subscribes.

Newsfeed

A newsfeed is established on the host computer using special software. A news administrator decides which newsgroups will be allowed through the newsfeed by subscribing to specific choices. All the users of the host computer can access the newsgroups that come through the newsfeed using newsreader software. Newsgroups are more efficient than electronic conferences (listservs or mailing lists) in that multiple users access one newsfeed instead of each user having an individual flow of messages to and from his or her own e-mail account. This saves disk storage space on the host computer system.

Newsgroups

Newsgroups are similar to e-mail discussion lists in that a user reads posted messages (called articles) and posts new messages or articles. They are different from e-conferences in that the host computer has one subscription to a newsgroup, then the individual users establish their own subscriptions to the host's. If the host does not subscribe to a newsgroup, you may request that the news administrator establish the subscription and allow the newsgroup through the newsfeed.

Newsgroups are arranged in broad categories (called hierarchies) such as these:

alt	Alternative/controversial, including topics such as sex
aus	Australia
biz	Business
can	Canada
comp	Computers and related issues
de	Germany
gov	Government
microsoft	Microsoft
misc	Miscellaneous topics that don't fit into the other categories
news	News about UseNet, including FAQs (frequently asked questions) and instructions for use
rec	Arts, hobbies, sports, and recreational activities
sci	Scientific topics
soc	Social issues and socializing
talk	Debates and long discussions

uk	United Kingdom
us	United States

These broad hierarchies are further subdivided into narrower topics of focus such as:

rec.sport.
    rec.sport.baseball
    rec.sport.fencing
    rec.sport.olympics (and several others)

soc.culture.
    soc.culture.china
    soc.culture.jewish
    soc.culture.nordic

Some e-mail discussion lists are also available through UseNet newsfeeds. You can spot messages from e-mail lists because they do not have the hierarchical names, and they may be lists with which you are familiar, such as: BusLib-L or LibRef-l.

DejaNews

The fastest and easiest way to get a taste of just what UseNet News is all about, without worrying about access to a server with a newsfeed, is to visit the DejaNews Website at http://www.dejanews.com. DejaNews offers the following definition of UseNet:

> Founded as the UseNet electronic bulletin board seventeen years ago, IDGs [Internet Discussion Groups] share the Internet's philosophy of openness: no one is "in charge" of them. Discussion groups are maintained on special "newsservers" all around the world, using a series of Internet standards and protocols. Newsserver sites pass IDG content back and forth, enabling anyone to read the content online using newsreader software, Web-based browsers with news reading capability, or Web-based search engines such as DejaNews.

You connect to DejaNews by opening its URL through your Web browser. After attaching to its Web page, you can search newsgroups by keyword and "lurk" anonymously or participate by responding through the DejaNews interactive response form. In the following exercise you will explore UseNet through DejaNews.

EXERCISE

This exercise works with both Netscape and Internet Explorer.

1. open the URL **http://www.dejanews.com**

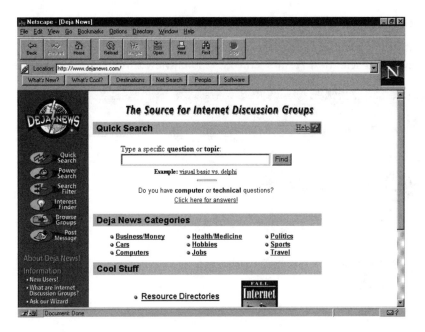

HINT   *The Quick Search text box offers the instructions: Type a specific question or topic.*

2. in the **search** text box, type: **library automation**

3. click on the **Find** button

Your search results look like this:

4. click on any **subject link** to read the entire message

   Notice your choices for managing the articles to which you matched:
   previous article, next results, current results, view thread, and post message.

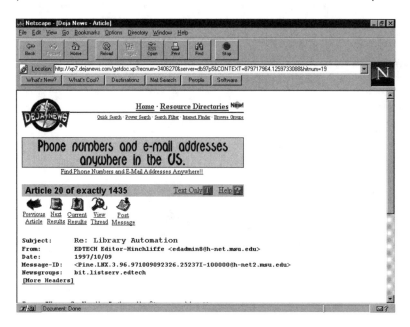

HINT

A thread *is a group of messages sharing the same subject
line, that is the common thread. When you choose to
View Thread you see the cluster of related messages.*

5. click on **Post Message** and you'll see a form to fill out to post responses
   to the newsgroup

6. fill in the fields and click on the **Submit Your Message** button

The bottom menu of the article page also allows you to send e-mail to the individual who posted the message/article rather than to the entire group.

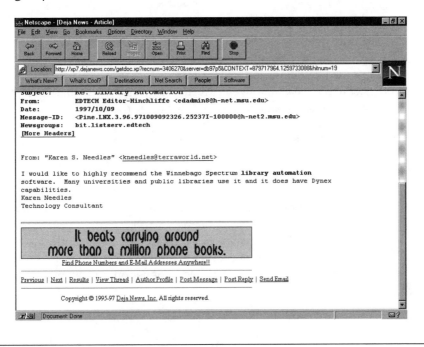

Newsreaders

The alternative to accessing UseNet through a Web page such as Deja-News is to use a newsreader. A newsreader is software on your host or local computer that enables you to read and create UseNet articles (messages). Unlike regular e-mail, anyone can read the UseNet articles you create.

There are several different newsreader softwares. Which one you use depends upon the type of host computer you use and the preference of your systems manager. A commonly used newsreader is called **rn** (for read news) and is for UNIX hosts. Another popular newsreader is called **nn**. You can access all the newsgroups to which your host computer subscribes or you may limit your access to a customized selection of groups to which you subscribe as an individual.

Why Try UseNet?

DejaNews, while being a handy service for exploring UseNet (or IDGs), aims itself at businesses that wish to identify target groups of potential consumers by monitoring discussions. Therefore, as quoted below, their opinion is extremely positive:

IDGs are so invaluable because they are the only medium that allows disparate groups of people with like interests to communicate on a world-wide scale. Any person in the discussion group can send a message to the entire group, and any of the other members can immediately respond to the entire group, too.

Then there are those who think most of UseNet is boring trash (including this author). UseNet is so broad, so voluminous, and so varied that it would be erroneous to write it off without a glance or to go to it looking for concise and reliable information. You must decide. So connect to the DejaNews Web page and search for topics that interest you: growing roses, making wine, or howling at the moon. You are sure to find some messages that match. Try posting an article; form your own opinion. Maybe there is some truly great information in alt.vampyres.

Warning

UseNet is not for the squeamish. Many participants have no interest in political correctness, or good manners, or objectivity. If you are assisting a library user who is researching a sensitive topic such as the Holocaust, be aware that you may encounter points of view that are offensively different from yours. Not all valuable information is palatable.

CHATTING ON THE INTERNET: VIRTUAL CONVERSATION

Almost weekly, it seems, we read a newspaper article or watch a news broadcast about innocents meeting predators through Internet chat rooms. Sadly, that is one possible abuse of this utility. Chatting is also used for harmless socialization, business meetings, and research, but these uses don't make the headlines.

Chatting on the Internet is made possible by a software utility called Internet Relay Chat (IRC). IRC is a client/server software. There are about 100 active IRC servers on the Internet that can carry chat transmissions from one to another, allowing conversations between individuals on opposite sides of the earth. The client piece of IRC is the software installed on your own computer that allows you to access IRC servers and initiate and organize conversations in cyberspace. IRC clients have various names such as mIRC, Netscape Chat, and Microsoft Comic Chat.

Finding, Installing, and Using Yahoo Chat

EXERCISE

This exercise works with both Netscape and Internet Explorer.

1. start your browser

2. open the URL: **http://chat.yahoo.com**

3. you see the Yahoo Chat page:

```
Welcome to Yahoo! Chat - Microsoft Internet Explorer          _ 5 x
File   Edit   View   Go   Favorites   Help
 ⇐      ⇒      ⊗     🔄    🏠     🔍      📷▾     🖨     A⁺    📥▾    📝                          e
Back  Forward  Stop  Refresh  Home  Search  Favorit...  Print  Font  Mail  Edit

Address http://chat.yahoo.com                                              ▾  Links
```

> **What's Happening In Yahoo! Chat?**
>
> - Monday, November 17: **Robert Newman** of "**Guiding Light**", at 6pm PT/9pm ET.
> - Monday, November 17: **Mike Vernon**, goalie for the San Jose Sharks, at 6pm PT/9pm ET.
> - New TV Rooms for all the big shows!
> - Get stock quotes while you chat in our **Stocks and Investments** room!
> - Habla Espanol? Check out our **Spanish-speaking** roooms!
> - New **health** and **support/recovery** rooms!
> - **....more Yahoo! Chat events here!**

New User?   **Used Yahoo! Chat Before?**

REGISTER WITH YAHOO! AND SET UP YOUR CHAT IDENTITY   ENTER YOUR

INSTALLING YAHOO CHAT SOFTWARE

1. click on the **Get the Software** button in the **New User** section

2. select your operating system in the list box provided

3. select your Internet browser from the list box provided

4. click on the **Go to Download Page** button

5. read the download and installation instructions provided

6. click on the **Click Here to Download** link

7. choose your **C:\busy** folder to receive the downloaded file

8. wait for the download to complete

9. **exit** all active programs

10. open **Windows Explorer**

11. locate the **busy** folder on the **C:** drive

12. double-click on the **busy** folder to open it

13. locate the **ichat** application file you just downloaded

HINT   *The file may have a name like* icnsyahoo220.

14. double-click on the **ichat** application file to launch the automatic installation

First, the installation Wizard is installed.

15. read each screen of the Wizard carefully and click on the **Next** button when you are done reading

16. when ichat setup is complete, **exit** Windows Explorer

4. click on the **Get Registered Now** button

5. in the **ID** box, enter a pseudonym for yourself

6. enter your information in the boxes provided

HINT   *Gender information is required, and if someone else is using the name or password you choose, you are prompted for another.*

7. read the **Terms and Conditions** that prohibit inappropriate behavior

8. click on the **I Accept** button; you'll see a list of topics you can choose to chat about

9. click on the **radio** button next to **Entertainment**

10. click on the **Start Chatting** button; examine the names of the various rooms under Entertainment

11. try clicking on a **room** link

12. follow the chat of those already in the room and try to determine if they are discussing anything of interest to you

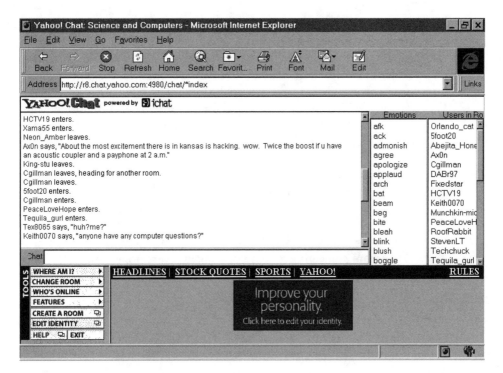

13. if you wish to contribute, enter your dialog in the **Chat** text box

14. examine the **Tools** window, and change rooms if you wish

> **HINT**   *The Help feature tells you how to put emotion into
> your chat text or speak privately to one individual.*

You are chatting in cyberspace. Don't worry, it's very obvious how to exit.
You'll have to draw your own conclusions about the value of IRC.

CASTING A GLANCE BACK

Don't just think about it anymore. If you haven't subscribed to an e-mail
discussion list, do it now. If your specialty is reference, try LibRef-L; if
you are a law librarian, it's LawLib-L; if you want to discuss anything
about public-access computers in libraries, then PACS-L is for you. Not
sure what I'm talking about? Take a look at the first couple of pages of
this chapter and get a refresher.

Once you subscribe to an e-mail discussion list, messages from other subscribers appear in your in-box every day. You can get in touch and stay in touch with hundreds, even thousands of individuals in your fields of interest and expertise from all over the world. Ask a question, and you are likely to be overwhelmed with a wide variety of answers, many of which will be helpful and some of which may be positively illuminating. If you don't like the list to which you subscribe, you can sign off and choose another.

E-mail between individuals is rapidly becoming a preferred method of communication. Get savvy about netiquette and brush up on your spelling and vocabulary, and you may find yourself checking your e-mail far more than your answering machine or voice mail.

As for UseNet and Chat, you may find them an enhancement to your personal hobbies and interests. Certainly UseNet is a method of researching uncensored opinions about every topic under the sun. Chatting is a sure way to find and provoke discussion about a wide variety of subjects. It could be gratifying to find some beneficial purpose for both.

Telnet: Your Key
to Remote Access

Telnet is the TCP/IP application that allows you to sign on to another computer and use its programs and network connections. Your computer acts as a virtual terminal, and you experience the remote computer as if it were sitting in front of you. Some computers do not allow you to open a Telnet session unless you have already established an account on that computer and have a login name and password. Many computers allow public-access Telnet. Several libraries with online catalogs allow public access remotely via Telnet. You may also use Telnet to access your account on a mainframe computer or a LAN file server. Ask your mainframe system operator or your network manager if this option is available to you.

Telnet makes your personal computer "dumb down," or emulate, a terminal. Terminals existed before desktop personal computers. A terminal is essentially a monitor and keyboard that share the processor or "brain" of a mainframe, or equivalent, computer. When you run Telnet, you are asking your computer to forget that it has its own processor, or brain, and to act like a terminal that depends upon the processor of a remote computer. This activity is called *terminal emulation*.

Digital Equipment Corporation (DEC) developed and manufactures the most popular terminals. Therefore, they set the standard for other terminal manufacturers. Some of the most commonly used terminals were the DEC VT100 and VT3270; therefore, there are now two popular types of terminal emulation: VT100 and VT3270. Most Telnet applications default to VT100 but have the option of switching to VT3270. Which emulation you need depends upon the site to which you are connecting. VT100 will work for most. There are other modes of emulation as well, which some Telnet applications support and some don't, for example, VT 320 and VT 420.

In addition to the individual postings you see sprinkled throughout the professional literature and electronic conferences, you can find Web pages that point you to Telnet sites such as Some Interesting Telnet Sites (http://www.cosy.sbg.ac.at/doc/eegtti/eeg_96.html#SEC97).

Library online catalogs are some of the most-preferred sites to which you can connect via Telnet. Therefore, the following exercises focus on visiting library catalogs.

TELNET THROUGH YOUR BROWSER

As stated throughout this book, it is desirable to use your Web browser as an all-purpose interface whenever possible. You can perform Telnet through your browser by constructing a URL out of the Telnet address you already know or by connecting to a Web page that offers links to Telnet sites. Either way, your browser is activating a Telnet program that exists outside it. The best way to understand this is to do a quick Telnet exercise.

SETTING UP NETSCAPE TO PERFORM TELNET

HINT   *If you are running Netscape 4.x, it will automatically find the Telnet application that comes with your Windows 95 or NT operating system.*

If you are running Netscape 3.x, you have to tell Netscape where the Telnet application is. To do so, complete these steps:

1. click on **Options**

2. click on **General Preferences**

3. click on the **Apps** folder tab

4. click on the **Browse** button next to the **Telnet Application** text box

5. locate the Telnet application in the **C:\windows** directory

HINT   *If you are on a network, you may find your Telnet application on another drive, such as **F:**. Ask your LAN manager for help.*

6. click on the **Telnet Application** to select it

7. click on the **Open** button

You should see the directory path and filename in your **Apps** (applications) window:

You are now ready to Telnet through Netscape!

EXERCISE

This exercise works with both Netscape and Internet Explorer.

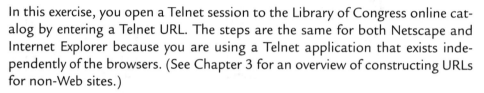

HINT   *If you begin this exercise in Netscape and receive an* Unable to find application *or similar error message, see the Setting up Netscape to Perform Telnet section in this chapter.*

In this exercise, you open a Telnet session to the Library of Congress online catalog by entering a Telnet URL. The steps are the same for both Netscape and Internet Explorer because you are using a Telnet application that exists independently of the browsers. (See Chapter 3 for an overview of constructing URLs for non-Web sites.)

1. open the URL: **telnet://locis.loc.gov**

2. press the **ENTER** key

```
Telnet - locis.loc.gov                                        _ □ ×
Connect  Edit  Terminal  Help
READY:
          L O C I S :  LIBRARY OF CONGRESS INFORMATION SYSTEM

          To make a choice: type a number, then press ENTER


   1   Library of Congress Catalog        4   Braille and Audio

   2   Federal Legislation                5   Organizations

   3   Copyright Information              6   Foreign Law

   *     *     *     *     *     *     *     *     *     *     *

   7   Searching Hours and Basic Search Commands
   8   Documentation and Classes
   9   Library of Congress General Information
  10   Library of Congress Fast Facts
  11   * * Announcements * *



  12   Comments and Logoff
       Choice:
```

You are connected to the Library of Congress site.

3. type **1** and press the **ENTER** key to access the online catalog

4. type **3** and press the **ENTER** key for "Books cataloged since 1975"

5. type **b white fang** to browse the catalog for *White Fang*

6. type **b#** (substituting an actual record[s] number for the #)

7. press the **ENTER** key

8. examine the record(s)

9. type **bye** to return to the Main Menu

10. type **12** to logoff

11. type **12** again to complete the logoff

12. close your Telnet window

Congratulations. You completed Telnetting through your browser.

HYTELNET: TELNETTING THROUGH A WEB PAGE TO LIBRARY CATALOGS

"HYTELNET is the utility which gives . . . a user instant-access to all Telnet-accessible library catalogs." The original version of HYTELNET was written by Peter Scott of Saskatchewan, Canada, for IBM PCs, but others have modified his program to create versions that run on other types of computers. For more information about HYTELNET, visit its Information Page at http://www.lights.com/hytelnet/.

One of the easiest ways to use HYTELNET is through the EINet Galaxy page at http://www.einet.net/hytelnet/START.TXT.html.

This exercise works with both Netscape and Internet Explorer.

1. open the URL: **http://www.einet.net/hytelnet/START. TXT.html**

The page to which you connect may look like this:

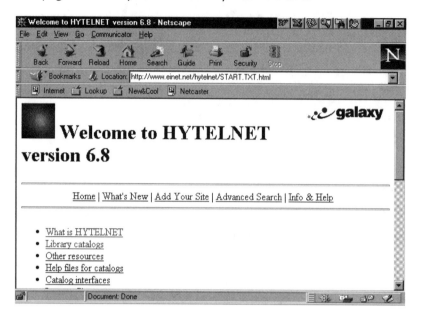

2. click on the **Library Catalogs** link

3. click on the **The Americas** link

4. click on the **United States** link

5. click on the **Other Libraries** link

6. scroll down through the extensive list until you find the **LOCIS: Library of Congress Information System** link and click on this link

You see a screen like this:

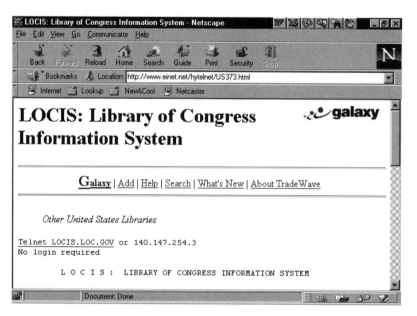

7. click on the **Telnet LOCIS.LOC.GOV** link

   Note how your browser automatically launches your Telnet application.

8. type **1** and press the **ENTER** key to access the online catalog

9. type **3** and press the **ENTER** key for "Books cataloged since 1975"

10. type **b white fang** to browse the catalog for *White Fang*

11. type **b#** (substituting an actual record[s] number for the #)

12. press the **ENTER** key

13. examine the record(s)

14. type **bye** to return to the Main Menu

15. type **12** to logoff

16. type **12** again to complete the logoff

17. close your Telnet window

Now take some time to explore Telnetting to some other library catalogs. Note that the HYTELNET Web page offers you instruction for logging on if an account name or password is required.

TELNETTING WITHOUT A BROWSER THROUGH WINDOWS 95 OR NT

When you use Telnet through your browser, you are actually launching a Telnet application that can function independently of your browser. If you don't want to fuss with a browser, you can go directly to the Telnet application and launch it.

Windows 95 and NT include a Telnet application as part of the standard package of Microsoft utilities. Because you are expected to activate this application through a browser, you won't find a shortcut icon for it or its name under the Programs folder, but you can still use it outside your browser. Simply follow the steps in the next exercise.

1. click on the **Start** button to pull down its menu

2. click on **Run**

HINT   *The Run selection allows you to start applications that do not appear on the Start menu or that have a shortcut on the desktop.*

You should see the Run dialog box:

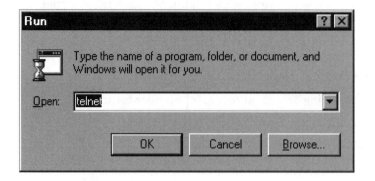

3. in the **Open** text box, type **telnet**

4. click the **OK** button

You should see the Telnet application window:

5. click on the **Connect** menu heading

6. click on the **Remote** menu item

You should see the Connect dialog box:

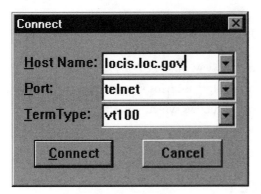

7. click in the **Host Name** box and enter the address **locis.loc.gov**

8. click on the **TermType** list box and note that the only terminal types available are VT100 and DEC-VT100; leave the selection at VT100

9. click on the **Connect** button

    You should soon connect to the Library of Congress catalog.

10. type **1** and press the **ENTER** key to access the online catalog

11. type **3** and press the **ENTER** key for "Books cataloged since 1975"

12. type **b white fang** to browse the catalog for *White Fang*

13. type **b#** (substituting an actual record[s] number for the #)

14. press the **ENTER** key

15. examine the record(s)

16. type **bye** to return to the Main Menu

17. type **12** to logoff

18. type **12** again to complete the logoff

19. close your Telnet window

    You just completed Telnetting outside your browser.

GETTING ANOTHER TELNET APPLICATION

You may need a Telnet application other than the one that comes with Windows 95 or NT, either because you are not using 95 or NT or because you need another terminal emulation besides VT100. You can download Telnet applications from a variety of sources. Talk to your

ISP or a local support person about which Telnet application is right for you. Here are some URLs for Telnet programs:

CRT	http://www.vandyke.com/vandyke/
NetTerm	http://starbase.neosoft.com/
TeraTerm	http://tucows.syracuse.net/term95.html#tera

TOTALING UP TELNET

Telnet allows your computer to act like a dumb terminal and connect to a remote server on the Internet. After connecting you can run programs on that server, such as a library's online catalog or a computer game.

There are a variety of terminal types that Telnet can emulate; the most common type is VT100. Others include VT 220, 320, and 420. Unless otherwise directed, VT100 should work for most purposes.

You can Telnet through your Web browser by putting a Telnet address into a URL with the prefix, telnet://. Telnet links are also found on Web pages. HYTELNET is an example of a Web site established solely for the purpose of Telnetting to library online catalogs. You can run a Telnet application outside your browser as well. Because you are actually running programs on someone else's computer, you may need to enter a user name or password to successfully complete your Telnet connection.

Eventually, as everything migrates to hypertext on the World Wide Web, Telnet may become obsolete. However, for now, it's the next best thing to being there.

FTP: Millions of Files
at Your Fingertips

FTP, or File Transfer Protocol, part of the TCP/IP suite, allows you to locate files on a remote server on the Internet and *get* or *download* them to your local computer so you can use them. Thanks to FTP you have access to millions of files of all types from all over the world. For example, say that you read about a librarian making her bibliographic instruction course outline and handouts available via FTP on the Internet. In minutes (with the correct address, file path, and file name) you can be downloading this course to your own computer for your own use. Librarians also use FTP to download software upgrades from a vendor's FTP site and to send and receive important files, such as cataloging databases and statistical reports.

In chapter 3 you learned how to easily download files from Web sites using the Save As features of your browser. This type of file retrieval may eventually eclipse FTP, but for now FTP is still used regularly for both file downloads and uploads.

TYPES OF FILES

Before you launch right into obtaining a plethora of free files, there are some basics you need to know. There are two types of files you transfer: text (or ASCII) and binary. You can often determine what the file type is by its extension. For a fantastic overview of file types found on the Internet connect to Common Internet File Formats at http://www.matisse.net/files/formats.html.

Text or ASCII files are generic files containing text that can be read by any word processing software or text editor. These files usually have a .txt extension.

Binary files are either archived/compressed ASCII text files that were shrunk to facilitate faster downloads or graphical (picture) files or program files or files formatted by a specific program such as WordPerfect or Lotus.

FTP THROUGH A WEB BROWSER

One of the many exciting aspects of your Web browser is that you can use it as an all-purpose interface to connect to any kind of server on the Internet. Your Web browser is not limited to connecting you to only World Wide Web servers. (See chapter 3 for more details about Web browsers.)

Your browser can open text files so that you may examine them before you download them. If your browser cannot open a file, it is a binary file.

ANONYMOUS FTP

Most FTP servers will allow anyone to connect and get files. The majority of FTP servers require that a user log on with a user name and password. Anonymous FTP server sites allow users to use the generic username of *anonymous* and their Internet address as a password. Your browser automatically provides the anonymous FTP information for you.

Anonymous FTP through Netscape

EXERCISE

You need a *busy* folder on the C: drive to complete this exercise as recommended. See Making an Exercise Directory for instructions on creating this folder.

In this exercise you will access Project Gutenberg. Project Gutenberg is a nonprofit volunteer project to get as much literature as possible into machine-readable form. The available texts can be retrieved using anonymous FTP.

1. start **Netscape**

2. open the URL for the Project Gutenberg FTP site: **ftp://uiarchive.cso. uiuc.edu/pub/etext/gutenberg/**

3. scroll down to the folder **etext97**

4. double-click on **etext97** to open it

5. scroll down and locate the file **wtfng10.txt**

> **HINT** The .txt *extension on this file indicates that it is an ASCII text file. You see* wtfng10.zip *here as well, which is a binary file that is used later in this exercise.*

6. click on the **wtfng10.txt** link

   Because this is a text file, you can see the entire text of *White Fang* through your browser.

7. click on **File**, then **Save As**

8. select your **busy** folder on the **C:** drive

9. click on the **Save** button

   You now have the full text of *White Fang* stored on your hard drive.

   Don't leave the Project Gutenberg site.

> **HINT** *Nontext (binary) files may load in your browser as well. If they don't, you get the Unknown File Type dialog box.*

10. click on the link **wtfng10.zip**

    You see the **Unknown File Type** box.

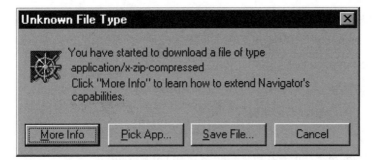

11. click on the **Save File** button; you see the **Save As** file dialog box

12. select your **busy** folder on the **C:** drive

13. click on the **Save** button

    You now have the binary zipped (compressed) *White Fang* stored on your hard drive. See Unzipping Files later in this chapter to learn how to unzip this file.

> **HINT** *If you know that you want to download a file without viewing it, hold down the SHIFT key while you click on the file. It will put you right into the Save As dialog box.*

Anonymous FTP through Internet Explorer

1. start **Internet Explorer**

2. type the URL for the Project Gutenberg FTP site in the **Address** box: **ftp://uiarchive.cso.uiuc.edu/pub/etext/ gutenberg/**

3. scroll down to the folder **etext97**

4. double-click on **etext97** to open it

5. scroll down and locate the file **wtfng10.txt**

HINT   *The .txt extension on this file indicates that it is an ASCII text file. You see* wtfng10.zip *here as well, which is a binary file that is used later in this exercise.*

6. click on the **wtfng10.txt** link

Because this is a text file, you can see the entire text of *White Fang* through your browser.

7. click on **File**, then **Save As File**

8. select your **busy** folder on the **C:** drive

9. click on the **Save** button

You now have the full text of *White Fang* stored on your hard drive.

Don't leave the Project Gutenberg site.

HINT   *Nontext (binary) files may load in your browser as well. If they don't, you get a dialog box.*

10. click on the link **wtfng10.zip**

Explorer appears to start downloading the file, but then it stops and gives you a warning box about viruses. The default choice is to save the file.

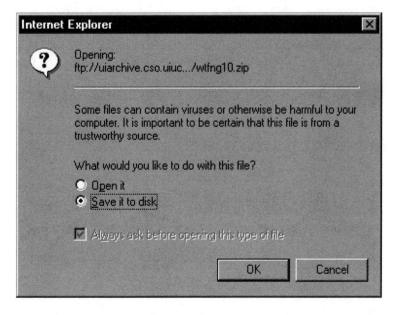

11. click on the **OK** file button; you see the **Save As** file dialog box

12. select your **busy** folder on the **C:** drive

13. click on the **Save** button

You now have the binary zipped (compressed) *White Fang* stored on your hard drive. See Unzipping Files later in this chapter to learn how to unzip this file.

RESTRICTED (NOT ANONYMOUS) FTP THROUGH NETSCAPE

You can perform FTP to and from computers on which you have an account. This is not anonymous FTP because you must have an account name and password to try it. Currently, restricted FTP cannot be done through Internet Explorer.

1. start your browser

2. open the URL for the FTP site on which you have an account

   Compose the URL as follows:

   ftp://accountname@host.subdomain.domain

   For example, I would gain FTP access to my account on a University at Albany computer with this URL: **ftp://murraylc@cnsvax.albany.edu.**

3. enter your **password** when prompted

4. press the **ENTER** key

   You see folders and file lists just as you do when you use anonymous FTP.

   You can actually upload, or send, files to a computer on which you have an account.

5. click on **File, Upload File**

6. click on the drive containing your files to upload

7. click on the files you wish to upload

8. click **OK**

   When the upload is complete, you receive a confirmation message.

FINDING FILES TO TRANSFER

In the previous anonymous FTP exercise, you were given the URL for the Project Gutenberg site and told where to find a file and what file to find. If you don't know where to go or what file you want, you can use a search engine devoted to searching anonymous FTP sites only.

In the very recent good old days, Archie (archive without a V) was your only tool for locating files available via anonymous FTP. Archie is a huge database that is an index of file directories from all the anonymous FTP servers it can query. It constantly updates itself. Several Archie servers index the files on more than a thousand other servers. You may search for files by name, directory, or a word in their text. Archie was terrific when it was the only game in town, but in comparison to the FTP search engines of Beaucoup, Snoopie, and Tile.Net (URLs listed below), it is not very user friendly. If you want to investigate Archie for historical purposes, you can connect to the URL for Archie Request Forms at http://www.nexor.com/archie.html.

Anonymous FTP search engines draw upon the Archie database, but they are easier to understand and use. Following is a list of FTP sites for you to explore. Keep reading for an up-close look at Snoopie File Search.

Beaucoup (Software)
   http://www.beaucoup.com/1softeng.html

Snoopie
   http://www.snoopie.com/

Tile.Net (FTP search page)
   http://tile.net/ftp-list/

Using Snoopie

This exercise works with both Netscape and Internet Explorer.

1. open the URL: **http://www.snoopie.com/**

   You should connect to the Snoopie File Search site.

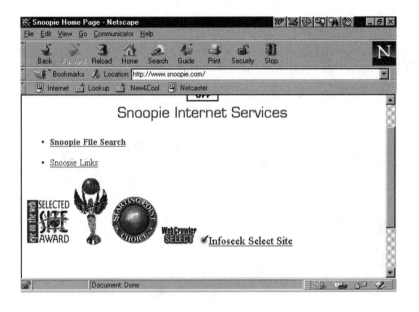

2. click on **Snoopie File Search**

3. in the **Enter Query** box, type **shakespeare**

   The list of results you see looks something like this:

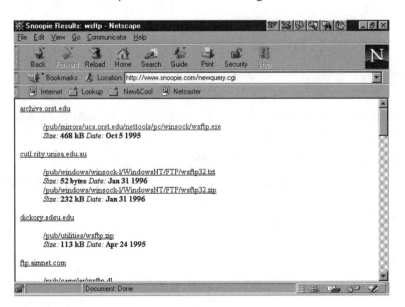

> **HINT** *The links that are flush with the left margin are for the general FTP site. The links that are indented lead directly to the directory or file that contains the keyword you are searching for.*

4. scroll down through the results list until you find the **Shakespeare Site: ftp://duke.cs.duke.edu/pub/ola/book/data/shakespeare/**

5. click on this link

> **HINT** *If you are denied access to the site, read the error message carefully. There may simply be too many people trying to log on anonymously at the same time, and you can try to connect again later.*

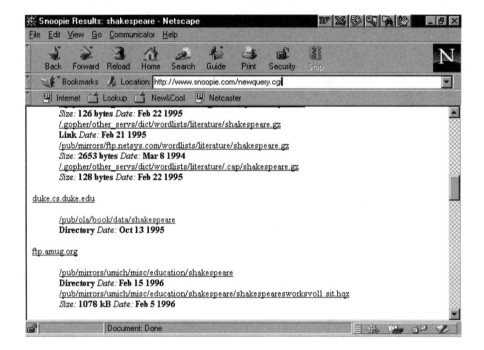

You connect to an FTP site at Duke University that contains the full text of some of Shakespeare's plays.

6. scroll down and locate the link **tempest**

You are now reading *The Tempest*. You may save this file if you wish, using the Save As instructions in the earlier exercises. Try it on your own if you are tempted.

FTP WITHOUT A WEB BROWSER

You may have a need to perform FTP without using a Web browser because you don't have a browser or because your task requires you to use the advanced features of an FTP application.

Downloading the WS_FTP Program

WS_FTP is a powerful yet friendly FTP application. You download WS_FTP as a single compressed file, then install it on your hard drive. In the following exercise, the program is compressed with PKWare. If you are not already familiar with PKWare and zipped files, skip ahead in this chapter and read all about it.

EXERCISE

This exercise works with both Netscape and Internet Explorer.

1. start **Windows Explorer**
2. open the **busy** folder on the **C:** drive
3. click on **File**, then **New**
4. click on **Folder** from the New menu

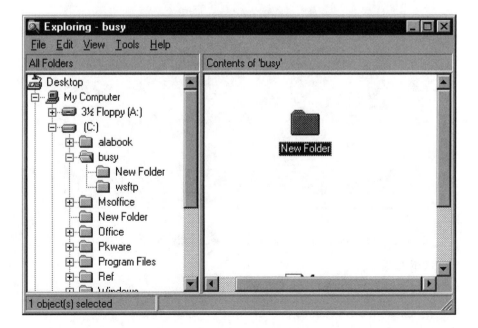

5. name the folder **WSFTP**

6. start your browser

7. open the URL **ftp://ftp.winsite.com/pub/pc/win95/netutil/**

8. the filename is **ws_ftp32.zip**; when you locate it, click on it

   You see the Unknown File Type box in *Netscape* or the file download dialog box in *Internet Explorer*.

File Download

Getting File Information:
ftp://ftp.winsite.com/p.../ws_ftp32.zip

File size unknown

Cancel

In *Internet Explorer,* this next dialog box appears:

Internet Explorer

? Opening:
ftp://ftp.winsite.com/p.../ws_ftp32.zip

Some files can contain viruses or otherwise be harmful to your computer. It is important to be certain that this file is from a trustworthy source.

What would you like to do with this file?

○ Open it
⦿ Save it to disk

☑ Always ask before opening this type of file

OK   Cancel

---

9. in *Internet Explorer,* click **OK** to proceed with the download

   OR

   in *Netscape,* using the **Unknown File Type** box

      click on **Save File** to proceed with the download

      you get a **Save As** dialog box

10. choose the **C:** drive, and the **WSFTP** folder that is under the **busy** folder as your destination

11. click the **Save** button, and your download proceeds

   Your download of the zipped WS_FTP file is complete. Good work.

Installing WS_FTP

In this exercise you unpack, or unzip, the file you downloaded in this previous exercise and install WS_FTP on your hard drive.

You don't need a browser for this one.

1. start **PKWare for Windows**

HINT	*See Unzipping Files later in this chapter for how to find and install PKWare for Windows.*

2. click on **File**, then **Open**

3. select the **C:** drive

4. open the **busy** folder, then the **WSFTP** folder

   You should see the **WS_FTP32.zip** file.

5. click on the file name

6. click on the **Unzip** file menu heading

7. click on **Extract files** from the menu

8. click on the **Done** button when it appears

9. **exit** PKWare

10. go to **Windows Explorer**

11. choose the **C:** drive

12. open the **busy** folder, then open the **WSFTP** folder

13. double-click on **Inst32** file

14. answer all the questions **yes**, and WS_FTP will install itself

Using WS_FTP

1. point to **Start**, **Programs**, **WS_FTP**, then **WS_FTP95 LE**

2. in the **Profile Name** box, type: **Gutenberg**

3. in the **Host_Name** box, type: **uiarchive.cso.uiuc.edu**

4. click on the **Anonymous Login** check box

5. click on the **Auto Save Config** check box

   Your WS_FTP connect window should look like this:

Session Profile	✕
Profile Name: Netscape ▼	Ok
Delete Save New	Cancel
Host Name: ftp.netscape.com	Advanced...
Host Type: Automatic detect ▼	Help
User ID: anonymous ☑ Anonymous Login	
Password: guest@unknown ☐ Save Password	
Account: ☑ Auto Save Config	
Initial Directories	
Remote Host:	
Local PC:	
Comment:	

6. click **OK**

   WS_FTP moves you to the next screen. Once you connect, your window looks like this:

7. double-click on the **pub** folder to open it

8. double-click on the **etext** folder

9. double-click on the **Gutenberg** folder

10. double-click on the **etext97** folder

    Look at the left window of WS_FTP. This is your local system. It is proba-
    bly showing the contents of your WSFTP folder on your C: drive.

11. double click on the **. .** twice

> **HINT**   *The two dots (. .) represent the folder/directory above*
> *the folder/directory you are in.*

Now you should see your **busy** folder.

12. double-click on the **busy** folder to open it

    Now look back at the right side of your WS_FTP window. This represents
    your remote system.

13. locate any file with a **.txt** extension and click on it

14. this is a text file; therefore, check your **ASCII** radio button

15. click on the **arrow** button pointing **left**, between the Remote window and
    the Local window

    Your file copies to the Local window and you see it in your **busy** folder.

COMMAND-LINE FTP

If you use the default FTP utility that comes with Windows 95 and NT or make your Internet connection through a mainframe, you may have to perform FTP at a command prompt.

The following general steps are those you follow when starting and using command-line FTP through Windows 95/NT:

1. obtain the FTP address, login instructions, and directory and file information
2. start FTP using the Run dialog box under the Windows Start menu
3. at your FTP prompt, type *open*, then the address of the host computer containing the files to transfer
   Wait for a message that says you are connected.
4. type a login name as instructed
5. type a password as instructed
6. list the files and directories; change into the directory you need
7. determine if the file you want is ASCII or binary and set the type
8. get the file(s)
9. decompress any compressed files

Commands for Command-Line FTP

ascii	sets the file type from binary to ASCII or TEXT on the host computer before transfer
dir	lists the files and directories on the remote FTP computer
binary	sets the file type to binary on the host computer before transfer
cd directory	changes into directories
cd /	changes back to the root or main directory
get filename	downloads the file to your computer using FTP
disconnect	disconnects from the remote host
quit	exits the Windows 95/NT FTP program

EXERCISE

1. in Window 95 or NT, click on the **Start** button in the Taskbar

2. click on the **Run** menu choice

3. in the dialog box provided, type **ftp** in the **Open** text box

Run	? ☒
🖳 Type the name of a program, folder, or document, and Windows will open it for you.	
Open:	ftp ▾
☐ Run in Separate Memory Space	
OK	Cancel	Browse...

4. click **OK**

5. at the ftp> prompt, type: **open uiarchive.cso.uiuc.edu**

6. press the **ENTER** key

7. at the **Name: (xxxxxx)** prompt, type: **anonymous**

8. press the **ENTER** key

9. at the **Password** prompt, type your e-mail address, for example: **yourusername@your.address<ENTER>**

 HINT   *You receive a screen of helpful messages, one of which tells you to read the file README.*

10. type **dir**

11. press the **ENTER** key

INTERPRETING A LIST OF FILES AND DIRECTORIES

Typing *dir* listed the names of the files and directories located in the root directory of the FTP host.

```
C:\WINNT\System32\ftp.exe                                        _ □ ×
230- - Joe Gross, Jason Wessel - Archive developers
230-
230-
230-Please read the file README
230-  it was last modified on Thu May 22 13:48:48 1997 - 198 days ago
230 Guest login ok, access restrictions apply.
ftp> dir
200 PORT command successful.
150 Opening ASCII mode data connection for /bin/ls.
total 6368
-rw-rw-r--   1 jgross   ftpadmin     423 May 22  1997 README
d--x--s--x   2 root     system       512 Jun  6  1995 bin
-rw-rw-r--   1 ftpadmin ftpadmin 2559242 Dec  6 17:53 du.out
d--x--s--x   3 root     system       512 May 30  1996 etc
lrwxrwxrwx   1 jwessel  ftpadmin      14 May 30  1996 index.html -> pub/index.
tml
drwxr-s---  14 ftpadmin 75           512 Jan 14  1997 licensed
drwxrwsr-x   8 ftpadmin ftpadmin     512 May 30  1996 local
-rw-rw-r--   1 ftpadmin ftpadmin 3949002 Dec  6 17:28 ls-lR.Z
drwxrwsr-x  18 ftpadmin ftpadmin     512 Dec  2 21:19 pub
drwxr-sr-x   2 root     ftpadmin     512 Dec  1 08:00 usage.stats
d--x--s--x   3 root     ftpadmin     512 Jun  6  1995 usr
226 Transfer complete.
722 bytes received in 1.42 seconds (0.51 Kbytes/sec)
ftp> _
```

As you read each entry from left to right, the following paragraphs explain columns on the screen.

The *first* character of the information string in the first column tells you if the item is a directory or a file:

- **d** = directory
- **l** = a link to another directory
- **-** = a file you can download

Directories are headings under which files are stored; they are not files themselves. They are organized in an inverted tree structure, with the root directory at the top level. You use the Change Directory or cd command to change in and out of them.

The remaining characters in the first column are codes designating the type and amount of access a user has to the item.

Columns 2, 3, and 4 contain miscellaneous identity information.

Column 5 is the size of the file in bytes (a byte is one character of information). The size given for directories does not indicate the byte size of the files stored in the directory, but rather the size of the directory structure itself.

Column 6 is the creation/modification date.

Column 7 is the creation/modification time.

Column 8 is the actual directory or filename.

12. type **cd pub** **<ENTER>**

FTP requires case sensitivity, *therefore you must type directory and file names exactly as they are listed, using the same capital and lowercase letters.*

13. type **dir**, press **ENTER**

14. type **cd etext**, press **ENTER**

15. type **dir**, press **ENTER**

16. type **cd gutenberg**, press **ENTER**

17. type **dir**, press **ENTER**

    Examine the list of files and directories in the **gutenberg** directory. Note the etext subdirectories divided by year.

18. type **cd etext94**, press **ENTER**

19. type **dir**, press **ENTER**

*If you have too many files to fit on one screen, you can use the <PAUSE> key to scan the list. If you know the name of the file, or part of the name, you can narrow the list down by using the * (wildcard character).*

20. type **get fdr10.txt** (President Franklin Delano Roosevelt's First Inaugural Speech)

21. press the **ENTER** key

22. wait until the **ftp>** prompt returns

23. type **disconnect**, press **ENTER**

24. type **quit**, press **ENTER**

    The file is downloaded to your local computer. You will probably find it on your desktop or in the root directory (C:) of your hard drive when you open Windows Explorer to look for it. Because fdr10.txt is a plain text file, you can open it in any word processor to read it.

UNZIPPING FILES

As noted before, you encounter a variety of file types on the Internet. It is inevitable that you come across files with .zip extensions. A zipped file is either a single large file that has been compressed for faster downloading and more efficient storage or multiple files that are grouped together and compressed under a single file name.

You can unzip a zipped file with PKWare for Windows. This is a shareware program that you can install on your own hard drive. The easiest way to get hold of PKWare is through its home page at http://www.pkware.com.

EXERCISE

This works with both Netscape and Internet Explorer.

1. launch your browser

2. open the PKWare URL: **http://www.pkware.com**

3. click on the PKZIP for Windows graphic that says **Download Shareware**

4. the next window you see gives you a choice of versions; click on the version that is correct for your computer

5. the next window offers you a variety of choices for downloading from different FTP sites; it is best to start with the first site, then move down through the list if you are unable to connect

> **HINT**   *Choose the 16-bit version of PKWare for Windows if you are using Windows 3.1. Choose the 32-bit version if you are using Windows NT, 95, or higher.*

6. when you connect successfully to one of the FTP sites, you may have to click again on the file name link to actually begin the download

    You receive an **Unknown File Type** dialog box in *Netscape* or a **file save** dialog box in *Internet Explorer*. Both lead you to the **Save As** dialog box.

7. click on the **Save** button

8. choose the **busy** folder on the **C:** drive as your destination

9. click on the **Save** button to start the download

10. when the download is complete, open **Windows Explorer**

11. open the **busy** folder on the **C:** drive

12. locate the PKWare file that you just downloaded (its name resembles this: **pk250w32.exe**)

13. double-click on the file name and PKWare walks itself through an automatic installation; all you have to do is click on the **Extract** button and answer **Yes** when it asks you about creating the PKWare directory

HINT   *After PKWare is installed you can start it and open the zipped file version of* White Fang, *which you downloaded in an earlier exercise (wtfng10.zip).*

14. click on the **Start** button, then point to **Programs**, then to the **PKWare** folder

15. point to the **PKZip for Windows** application, and PKWare is launched

16. click on the PKWare **File** menu

17. click on **Open File**

18. change to the **C:** drive and the **busy** directory

19. click the file you downloaded earlier: **wtfng.zip**

20. click on the **Open** button

    In the PKWare window you should see that the content of **wtfng.zip** is wtfng10.txt.

21. click on the **Unzip** menu heading

22. click on the **Extract files** choice

23. in the next window, click on the **Extract** button

HINT   *Because you may already have wtfng10.txt downloaded to your busy folder, you may get a dialog box asking you if it is OK to overwrite. Click on* **Yes**.

24. when the extraction is done, a **Done** button appears in the PKWare Window; click on the **Done** button

25. **exit** PKWare

    Excellent. Unzipping files is now one of the many cyber skills in your new repertoire.

FTP FINALE

There are many choices for using FTP: You can upload and download files through your favorite browser. You can use an FTP program under Windows such as WS_FTP, which allows you to create directories and rename files on both the local remote computers you are using (if you have the correct privileges, of course). You may also opt to type FTP commands at the command prompt of your account on a mainframe computer. The principles are the same, and the commands are readily mastered with practice.

Now that you know FTP, you do not have to wait for a disk with a software upgrade; ask the vendor if you may download it from the vendor's FTP site instead. If you are exchanging information with a government agency or another library, ask if FTP is a communication option. It cuts out the time and expense of transferring files using traditional methods (and impresses the heck out of the people with whom you are working).

Searching the Internet: A Chaotic New World for Librarians

8

The information explosion is nowhere more obvious than in the area of search sites on the World Wide Web. There are many sites; the many are varied; and the variations are numerous. The first challenge to using an Internet search site is casting away all expectations that you may be able to apply any search skills acquired using commercial database services such as Dialog, OCLC, Silverplatter, etc. Commercial databases use standardized subject headings, such as Library of Congress Subject Headings, and standardized record formats, such as MARC. Internet search sites use neither.

The second challenge is understanding the jargon that is particular to this arena. Sites devoted to searching the Internet are commonly called *search engines*. As with most common-usage titles, this label is not entirely correct. The search engine is the program that sweeps through information servers on the Internet, collects data about their resources, indexes the information, and allows you to query the resulting database using keyword searching or other access methods. Search sites consist minimally of the search engine software *and* the database of Internet resources it creates. Most search sites also offer browsable catalogs of resources organized under broad (nonstandard) subject headings. A search engine can be used to create and search databases for individual sites on the Web. For example, the ALA Web site uses Excite's search engine to index and locate information from its site. If you visit the Excite search site, you use the Excite search engine to search Excite's enormous database of Internet resources. From this point on, *search engine* is used interchangeably with *search site*.

The third challenge is recognizing familiar database-searching techniques and concepts disguised under unthreatening but (to the information professional) unfamiliar labels. For example, in the Yahoo Advanced Search Features "matches on all words" replaces the Boolean AND.

Before you jump into the mix of search site categories and evaluations, it would be wise to visit a small site, try some simple searches, analyze search results, examine the engine's features, and basically get comfortable with the entire concept. The following section and its exercise will help you do just that.

A WORD ABOUT WAIS

WAIS stands for Wide Area Information Server and is pronounced *ways*. WAIS servers contain databases of information organized by subject. The WAIS client (the part of the software designed to access the server) searches almost the entire text of each document in these databases for matches on keywords. Before Gopher and the World Wide Web, WAIS was the only tool for locating information by subject on the Internet. WAIS is only one of many searching options now available to Internet users; therefore, it has greatly diminished in popularity.

For more information about WAIS you can download an FAQ file from the FTP site at MIT: ftp://rtfm.mit.edu/pub/usenet/news.answers/wais-faq.

YAHOO: THE MANAGEABLE PLACE TO START

EXERCISE

This exercise works using both Netscape and Internet Explorer.

1. open the URL: **http://www.yahoo.com**

   When you connect you should see the memorable Yahoo logo.

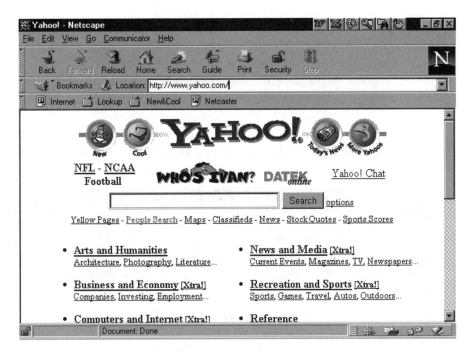

2. click in the **Search** text box

3. type in the search terms: **ready reference**

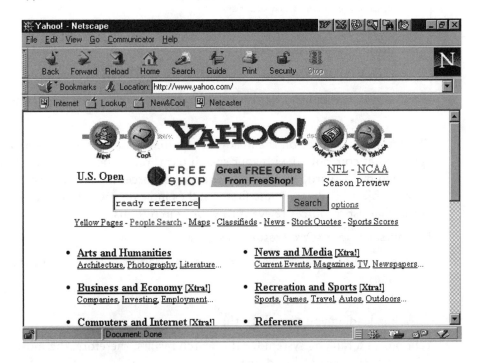

4. click on the **Start Search** button next to the text box

5. wait for Yahoo to process your search

> **HINT** *Many factors influence the length of time it takes to process your search: the speed of your connection, the amount of traffic on the Internet, the number of other users searching on the same site, and the number of hits or matches the search engine is finding for your search words.*

6. **scroll** down; you should see a list of hits that looks something like this:

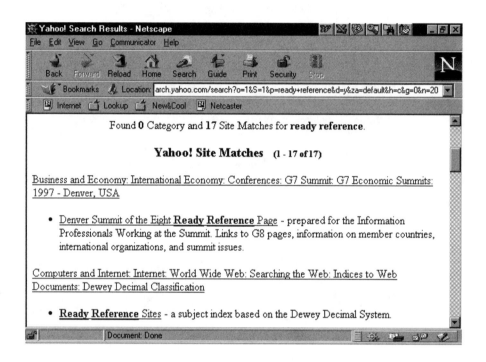

The first items you see on the list of hits (matches) are Yahoo subject categories that correspond with your search term. Yahoo not only allows you to search by keyword, you can also browse resources indexed under broad subject headings. These first matches indicate the subject categories that list resources relevant to your search terms.

In a nutshell, your search results give you

the name of a matched site (this is a link leading you directly to the site)

a description of the site

a link leading you directly to the site

Yahoo uses a ranking system for the search results; therefore, the most relevant sites *should* be listed first.

7. pick a link from your list of hits

8. click on the link

You should connect to the site described.

HINT   *If you are unable to connect to the match you chose,*
try another.

9. explore the site you chose; if it doesn't meet your needs, click on your
   BACK button to return to the **Search Results** screen to choose another
   link

Guess what? You are surfing the Internet.

Once you locate a relevant site, it usually leads you to related sites. In essence, you catch the wave and ride it out. OK, you've plunged in, grabbed the board, and caught the wave. Got that adrenalin rush out of your system? Good, because it is time for a quick overview of searching.

MORE ABOUT SEARCH ENGINES

Most search engines index World Wide Web information unless they are uniquely devoted to one specific type of information. Many search sites include records for other types of information such as FTP, Gopher, Telnet, and UseNet News.

Some sites contain more information in their databases than others. Yahoo's database is the smallest of all the general search engines, but it tries to compensate for its size by offering quality starting-point links. Lycos (http://www.lycos.com) claims to have the largest database and to cover over 90 percent of the Internet.

Searching Techniques

Search sites offer two levels of searching: simple and advanced. The simple search usually allows you to enter your keywords and click on a search button. The Boolean AND is often the default on a simple search. Advanced searching varies from site to site and may allow you to change the Boolean operators and to specify a range of dates, languages, types of data, and the format of your search-result display.

Advanced Searching in Yahoo

EXERCISE

This exercise works using both Netscape and Internet Explorer.

1. open the URL: **http://www.yahoo.com**

   When you connect, you should see the Yahoo logo:

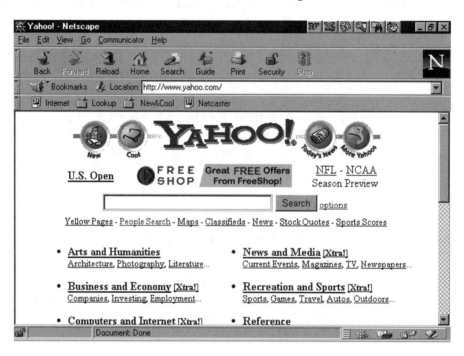

| **HINT** | *Next to the Search button is a link called <u>options</u>.* |

2. click on the **options** link

| **HINT** | *Note that you can narrow your search to just UseNet or e-mail.* |

3. examine the **search methods**

4. click on **an exact phrase match** choice

| **HINT** | *Exact phrase matches look for the words in the order you type them—immediately adjacent to each other. The* matches on all words (AND) *choice does* not *honor word order or adjacency.* |

5. examine **Select a search** area

Yahoo Categories limits you to records that are indexed by subject using subject headings developed just for Yahoo (as opposed to standardized subject headings such as those developed by the Library of Congress). Web Sites gives you access to the entire Yahoo database, which is assembled with automated search engine software.

6. click on **Web Sites**

7. click on the **list** box next to **Find only new listings added during the past** and examine the choices

8. leave the selection at **3 years**

9. leave the display at **20 matches per page**

10. scroll back up to the **Search** text box and type in your keywords: **ready reference**

Your advanced search window now resembles this:

11. click on the **Search** button to send your search

Your search results (below) are narrower than those of your first search due to choosing the exact phrase match.

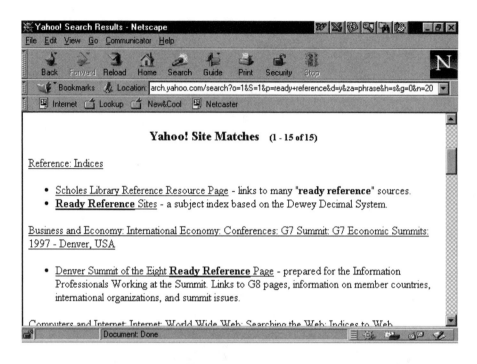

ALTAVISTA: THE CHALLENGE OF SEARCHING A MAJOR PLAYER

AltaVista is considered one of the major players in the current array of search engines. Its database of Internet resources is vast. Although it has an advanced search option that allows you to set a variety of limits on your search, you usually receive thousands of hits for all but the most specific or esoteric searches. You need to abandon any ideals of examining all the matches for your search words.

Don't worry about missing an important link at the bottom of your very long list of search results. The nature of the hyperlinked Internet environment is that sites that are related topically tend to point to each other. If it exists, you should find what you need within the first fifty to one hundred hits. If you don't find the information you seek after examining one hundred hits, you should try searching with some different search terms rather than continuing to slog through your original search results.

If you are ready to wrangle with a much larger dataset than Yahoo's, try the following hands-on exercise for AltaVista.

This exercise works using both Netscape and Internet Explorer.

1. open the AltaVista URL: **http://www.altavista.com**

   You see a screen like this:

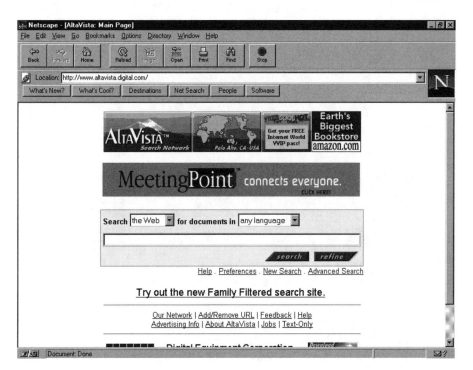

2. click on **Advanced Search**

3. click on the **Search** list box; note that you can search UseNet news articles as well

   HINT   *See chapter 5 for more about UseNet.*

4. leave the choice at **the Web**

5. click on the **any language** list box; note all the choices

6. click on **Help**; note the following:

HINT		*You enter your search in the blank text box below the Search and language text box.*

7. type the search words **ready reference**

8. click in the **Ranking** text box

9. type the search words **ready reference** again

10. in the **From** list box, enter the date **01/Jan/96**

11. in the **To** text box, enter **today's date** in the format dd/mm/yy

> **HINT**   *If you click* Give me only a precise number of matches, *you receive only a count of the matches for your search, not links to the actual records. The purpose of this option is to test your search query.*

Your advanced search screen should look something like this:

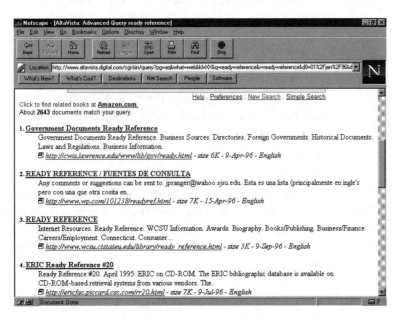

12. click on the **Search** button to submit your search terms

13. wait for a list of matches

HINT	*You'll probably receive more than 13,000 hits. You did not do anything wrong, and you may not be able to narrow your search any more. That is the nature of the large search engine beast. By using the Ranking choice, you should find that the most relevant sites appear first. Is it necessary to examine every record received in such an enormous number of search results? Probably not.*

You are now done with your advanced AltaVista search.

WHERE TO LEARN MORE ABOUT SEARCHING

There is a tremendous amount written about Internet search engines. Industrious people spend countless hours compiling, assessing, explaining, and evaluating the myriad of sites. Following are a few sites that compile links to search engines and explain and evaluate them. These sites give you the detailed information that helps you determine which sites best meet your searching needs. With so much from which to choose, you may want to get comfortable with a small, manageable site such as Yahoo and then wade in gradually to other sites.

The Best Search Engines
http://www.lookup.com/Homepages/73107/search.htm

Search Engine Watch
http://calafia.com/webmasters

Understanding and Comparing Web Search Tools
http://www.hamline.edu/library/bush/handouts/comparisons.html

Understanding WWW Search Tools
http://www.indiana.edu/~libresd/search/

You have already tried out Yahoo, the most immediately gratifying and easily used of all the search engines. There are dozens of others. For an overwhelming overview, you can visit a site such as Beaucoup (http://www.beaucoup.com/engines), which categorizes and compiles search sites.

This is Beaucoup's list of General Search Engines:

LinkStar	Excite	LinkMonster
New Rider's YP	Nexor's AliWeb	NetCenter
Lycos	Harvest Broker	REX
WebCrawler	Net Navigator	NlightN
AltaVista	Net Happenings	LEO
LinkMaster	URL Tree	Open Text
Infoseek	World Announce	Infohiway
Nerd World	Arch.	W5
Yahoo	WWWWorm	HotBot
Magellan	CUI W3 Catalog	i-Explorer
Inktomi	web://411	infoseek Ultra
Tradewave Galaxy	Pathfinder	Identify
Jayde	Tribal Voice	Intuitive Web Index

Beaucoup also has other categories for search engines that cover all types:

Multiple Engine Searches (some allow simultaneous searching of multiple engines)

Reviewed Sites/What's New? (reviews of Web sites and lists of new Internet resources)

Media (online newspapers and magazines)

Geographically Specific (search sites for places worldwide)

Software (search sites for software repositories)

TRY LYCOS ON YOUR OWN

After trying the smallest search engine, Yahoo, you may want to see what the biggest is all about. Visit Lycos (http://www.lycos.com) and try a few searches. You learn quickly that no matter how you try to narrow your search, you often receive thousands of matches. This enormous return of matches is common for most search engines. Luckily, you often find all the information you need in the first one hundred results.

DISTILLING IT DOWN

Search engines are a necessity, and everyone is glad to have them as a tool to locate resources on the Internet. They are also sorely in need of improvement and should turn toward the producers of commercial databases and follow their example by adopting standardized subject headings and search techniques. More and more search engine producers are hiring librarians to assist with indexing and categorizing resource records, and this trend can only be viewed as positive.

For now, information professionals must accept the reality of using search tools that offer an enormous variety of search techniques that usually result in an enormous amount of matches to a search query. The experienced searcher of commercial databases must shelve her or his skills and ego to use an Internet search engine.

To learn more about search engines, visit the sites listed above under Where to Learn More. You find that once you get comfortable using two or three sites, the process becomes less overwhelming. A good rule of thumb is: don't limit yourself to one search engine, but don't overwhelm yourself with more than three or four.

If librarians and information professionals become more involved in the creation and management of search engines, the future holds more organized and manageable methods of searching the Internet.

Gopher: Going, Going, Almost Gone

9

Gopher is a menu interface to the Internet that precedes the World Wide Web browser and is rapidly diminishing. Gopher is an example of client/server software. The server piece is installed and managed by the Gopher "owner," and the client piece is used to access the resources made available from the Gopher server. The Gopher server software allows the creation of menu choices that lead to files and services available on the Internet. As with the design of Web pages, the Gopher creator decides what Internet services users will want to use most frequently. Then he or she determines the way to access these services: FTP, Telnet, etc. Next, a link script is built that contains the instructions for connecting to the service. When a Gopher user chooses a menu option, these scripts activate and make the connection. Following is an example of a Gopher link script:

Type=11.Electronic Conferences for Librarians
Name=Electronic Libraries
Path=/libraries/elibraries
Host=gopher2.ucls.edu
Port=70
URL:gopher://gopher2.ucla.ed:70/11/library/elibraries

The Gopher owner can edit and move Gopher menu selections at will; therefore, he can expand or contract the menu as necessary.

Most Gopher sites have been usurped by World Wide Web home pages. Institutions and individuals that maintain active Gopher sites usually also maintain Web pages that point to the active Gopher.

USING A GOPHER/LOCAL CLIENT

Some of you may still have access to a local Gopher client. If you work at a mainframe command prompt, you may connect to your home Gopher by simply typing gopher and pressing ENTER. If you have a Windows (or Macintosh) Gopher client, you can identify your Gopher client by looking for an icon of a buck-toothed gopher. Once you find the rodent, double-click on it. Your home Gopher is either a local or remote Gopher that your Gopher manager has established as the default to which you connect. If you know the address of a remote Gopher, you may use your Gopher client to connect to it directly.

After connecting to your home Gopher you can quickly identify how the menus work and what it takes to navigate through them. The bottom of every Gopher screen explains navigation commands. Your primary challenge is deciding where to begin. Gopher menu conventions are

/   leads to another menu of options

.   accesses a file for you using an appropriate utility such as FTP

<?>   leads to an index search server and you are asked to enter a key word for searching

GOPHER COMMANDS

Typing *m* allows you to specify an e-mail address to which you want to send a text file you are reading on a Gopher. The *D* key (which must be a capital) downloads a text file you are reading on a Gopher. You are asked to specify a download protocol and must know how to activate your telecommunications software to receive a download.

You can review Gopher Help any time by typing a question mark. *Bookmark* is a handy Gopher command that carries over into Web browsers. When you find a Gopher menu item that you will want to use again, just type the letter *a* with your selection arrow pointing at the item. The selection is added to your own custom menu of bookmarks that you may retrieve by typing the letter *v* (for view).

GOPHERING THROUGH A BROWSER

If you do not have a Gopher client, or do not care to fuss with one, you can easily connect to a Gopher site through a Web browser. There are very few up-to-date Gophers left on the Internet; among them is the Library of Congress MARVEL Gopher site.

This exercise works using both Netscape and Internet Explorer.

1. start your browser

2. open the URL: **gopher://marvel.loc.gov**

 HINT   *Browsers automatically supply only the http:// prefix or scheme for a URL. Any other prefix such as Gopher:// must be typed.*

When you connect, you should see the Library of Congress Gopher menu:

```
Netscape - [gopher://marvel.loc.gov/]                                    _ 🗗 ✕
File  Edit  View  Go  Bookmarks  Options  Directory  Window  Help

  ⇦        ⇨       🏠        ⊗       📷       📰       🖨       🔍        ⬤
 Back   Forward   Home    Reload   Images    Open    Print    Find      Stop

  Location: gopher://marvel.loc.gov/                                 ▾      N
  What's New?   What's Cool?   Destinations   Net Search   People   Software
```

Gopher Menu

☐ About LC MARVEL
☐ Events, Facilities, Publications, and Services
☐ Research and Reference (Public Services)
☐ Libraries and Publishers (Technical Services)
☐ Copyright
☐ Library of Congress Online Systems
☐ Employee Information
☐ U.S. Congress
☐ Congressional Budget Office Gopher
☐ Government Information (no longer maintained)
☐ Global Electronic Library (no longer maintained)
☐ Internet Resources
☐ What's New on LC MARVEL
☐ Search LC MARVEL Menus

```
 🛣🖼   gopher://marvel.loc.gov:70/11/services                            📧?
```

A Web browser displays a Gopher menu differently than a Gopher client. For example

yellow folder	*leads to another menu of options*
dog-eared page with writing	*accesses a file for you using an appropriate utility such as FTP*
blank dog-eared page	*leads to an index search server where you are asked to enter a keyword for searching*
computer monitor with keyboard	*represents a Telnet link*

When connecting to a Gopher server through a Web browser, you are not able to use the standard Gopher commands noted earlier in this chapter. Gopher's help menu is not accessible through a Web browser. You can use the browser's bookmark command to bookmark Gopher sites as well as Web addresses. Instead of a capital D to download files, click on your browser's File pull-down menu and click on Save As or Save As File. Managing Gopher sites through a browser is not terribly different from managing Web sites.

3. click on **What's New on LC MARVEL**

 The dog-eared page icon with writing indicates links to actual documents.

4. click on your browser's **Back** button

5. click on the **Employee Information** link

 The blank page icon indicates that the Staff Telephone directory is a link to a database that you can search by keywords.

6. explore on your own

You have just gone gophering.

GOPHERS FACE EXTINCTION

Even active Gophers, such as MARVEL, are facing an inevitable demise at the hands of that ubiquitous hypertext predator: the World Wide Web. When you do encounter Gopher sites in your exploration of the Internet, check them carefully for currency. If a Gopher points you to a corresponding Web site—go there. Almost all current Gophers can be accessed through Web pages. Quite soon that simple, friendly Gopher menu, so useful in its time, will be just a page in the history of the Internet.

EPILOGUE

Now that you have worked your way through this book, you should have reached some level of comfort when using the Internet. No single person can know all there is to know about this vast cyberculture. Focus your continuing education on concepts and skills for which you have daily needs. Find an easily accessible magazine or online resource that keeps you up to date with Internet advancements and new resources. Ask questions and try things out. Real life is a great teacher.

Laura K. Murray is currently a library automation specialist for the State University of New York Office of Library and Information Services. Previously, she was an Internet and online reference specialist for the SUNY/OCLC Network. Laura is also an adjunct professor for the Information Science and Policy School of the University at Albany in New York. She created *The Internet Homesteader* journal and edited it from 1994 to 1997.